INTRODUCING TREES

INTRODUCING
Trees

AUTHOR: Pamela M. Hickman

ILLUSTRATOR: Judie Shore

Pembroke Publishers Limited

Pembroke Publishers
538 Hood Road
Markham, Ontario L3R 3K9

Canadian Cataloguing in Publication Data

Hickman, Pamela
  Introducing trees

(Hands on nature)
ISBN 0-921217-91-9

1. Trees – Study and teaching (Elementary).
I. Shore, Judie. II. Federation of Ontario
Naturalists. III. Title. IV. Series

QK75.H53 1992   372.3'57   C92-094819-7

Advisors: Dr. Kevin Kavanagh,
          Botanist, World Wildlife Fund Canada
        Pam Crosby,
          Teacher, York Region Board of Education

Editor: Lou Pamenter
Design: John Zehethofer
Cover Photography: Ajay Photographics
Typesetting: Jay Tee Graphics Ltd.

This book was produced with the generous assistance of the government
of Ontario through the Ministry of Culture and Communications.

For further information on the Federation of Ontario Naturalists and how
you can become a member contact:

FEDERATION OF
Ontario Naturalists
355 Lesmill Road. Don Mills. Ontario M3B 2W8 (416) 444-8419

Printed and bound in Canada
9 8 7 6 5 4 3 2 1

Contents

Introduction

Look around your classroom or any room at home and count the number of things you see that come from trees. No doubt your list will be long, but did you also include things like resins, paints, cork, rubber, carpeting, fabrics, cellophane, photographic film, buttons, combs, pillows, upholstery and even eyeglass frames? These products are also derived from trees.

Trees not only enhance our lifestyle but they are also an important part of our daily survival and vital components of natural ecosystems. As efficient oxygen producers, trees help to provide animals, including people, with the life sustaining element through photosynthesis. The same process uses up quantities of carbon dioxide in the air, helping to reduce the greenhouse effect. Trees also help reduce soil erosion, act as wind breaks, recycle water, and provide food and shelter for millions of plants, fungi, and animals.

Introducing Trees encompasses the basics of tree biology, how to teach about trees indoors and out, how trees affect our lives, and how people affect trees — positively and negatively.

Each chapter has an introductory backgrounder to give you the information needed for the concept of the chapter. The bulk of the chapter consists of a set of lessons, each based on several activities. Particular background is given to you at the beginning of each lesson. You may choose to do all the activities or pick out those that you feel are most appropriate for your classroom. Whichever choice you make, you will find that the activities provide the focus for the learning experience. In some cases, activities have an accompanying Student Activity Sheet that can be reproduced and given to the students. If the students keep their Activity Sheets together, they will have a comprehensive portfolio of facts about trees.

A large colorful poster is also available that is designed for classroom display. It can be particularly useful as a focus in a learning centre.

Introducing Trees will provide students with some of the basic building blocks of natural history knowledge. However, the activities use a broad, cross-curriculum approach so that you can teach about nature outside of a designated "science period". Students will be asked to observe, to communicate, to use mathematical skills, and to manipulate materials and equipment. In particular, students will be asked to observe a wide variety of trees, and their parts; to investigate similarities and differences; to find out what trees need to survive and what animals need trees for survival; to prepare oral and written presentations; to roleplay; and to draw and construct.

After all, respect for living things and interest in and care for the environment are attitudes that are part of every curriculum. They are attitudes that should permeate everyone's lifestyle. Trees are an important aesthetic part of our landscape, vital to our economy, and an almost legendary component of our natural heritage. We hope your students will enjoy learning about trees, and become committed to their conservation and wise use in the future.

The best way to start is to go outside and look at some trees. Have students talk about what they know about trees, and about things they'd like to know about trees. If you cannot get outside to view trees, use the tree poster as a focus for your conversation. Get everyone thinking about trees!

CHAPTER ONE

Meet a Tree

Ask your students to name some plants. Chances are most of the answers will be different kinds of flowering plants or common varieties of houseplants. Although trees are very familiar plants to most kids, they are often thought of as a separate entity. This introduction will show your class that trees and herbaceous or non-woody plants (including typical flowers), share many similar characteristics, but also have some differences that set them apart.

Take your class outdoors to observe some trees and flowers growing. If this is not possible, try to obtain a potted tree and flower for the classroom for observation. Ask each child to look at, and gently touch, the plants and list their general features. Don't forget to include the roots below ground even though they may not be visible. Record their answers in two columns: one headed TREES and the other headed HERBACEOUS PLANTS. Have students decide what features are common to both types of plants. Discuss the differences between trees and herbaceous plants.

These are characteristics of a general plant:

stem (trunk is a type of stem)
roots
leaves
flowers (cone-bearing trees, such as pine,
    spruce, fir don't have true flowers)
seeds/fruit

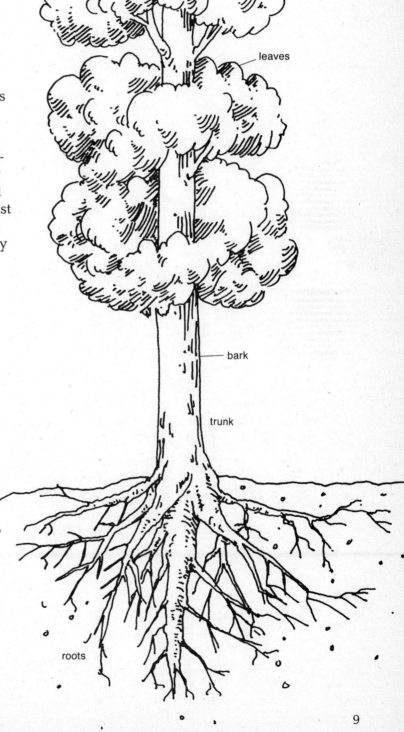

leaves

bark

trunk

roots

maple key

elm seed

TREES	HERBACEOUS PLANTS
trunk	stem
hard woody trunk	soft stem
leaves	leaves
flowers (may or may not have them)	flowers (may or may not be present)
roots	roots
bark	no bark
seeds and/or fruit (may or may not be present)	seeds and/or fruit (may or may not be present)
branches	branches (may not have them)

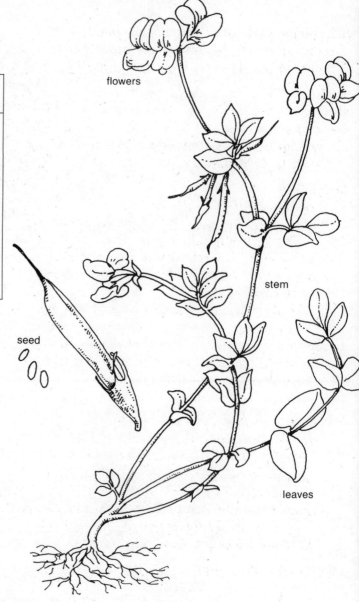

flowers

stem

seed

leaves

To summarize the differences between trees and herbaceous plants:

— trees are larger than herbaceous plants
— trees have thicker stems
— trees have harder, woody stems and branches
— a tree's leaves are usually larger
— trees have bigger roots

In general there are two major differences between trees and other plants: size and structure. Trees are bigger and are woody, not soft-stemmed. Shrubs are also woody plants but they tend to be smaller than trees and have more than one stem.

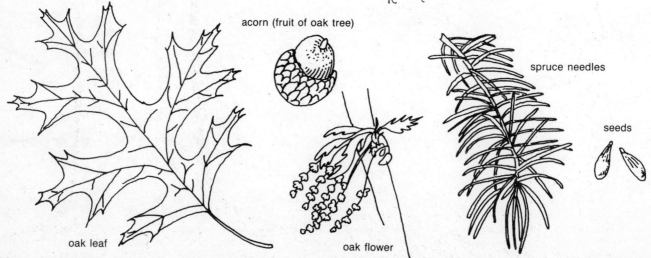

acorn (fruit of oak tree)

spruce needles

seeds

oak leaf

oak flower

The major parts of a tree, or any plant, — roots, stem and leaves — work together to help it grow. Here is a brief summary of their roles.

Roots
☐ anchor the tree
☐ take up water and minerals from the soil to feed the tree

Stem/trunk
☐ provides support to the tree
☐ contains the "plumbing" of the tree where water and minerals are carried from the roots up to the rest of the tree and sugars are carried from the leaves to other parts of the tree
☐ is the place where all other plant parts are attached
☐ a tree's outer bark is made of hardened, dead cells and serves to protect the tree from damage and disease

Leaves
☐ like a mini factory, leaves make food for the tree through a chemical reaction called photosynthesis. Chlorophyll — the green color in leaves — is necessary for the reaction to occur. Carbon dioxide from the air is combined with water from the roots, in the presence of sunlight, to produce sugar (glucose) and oxygen.

carbon dioxide + water → glucose + oxygen
sunlight

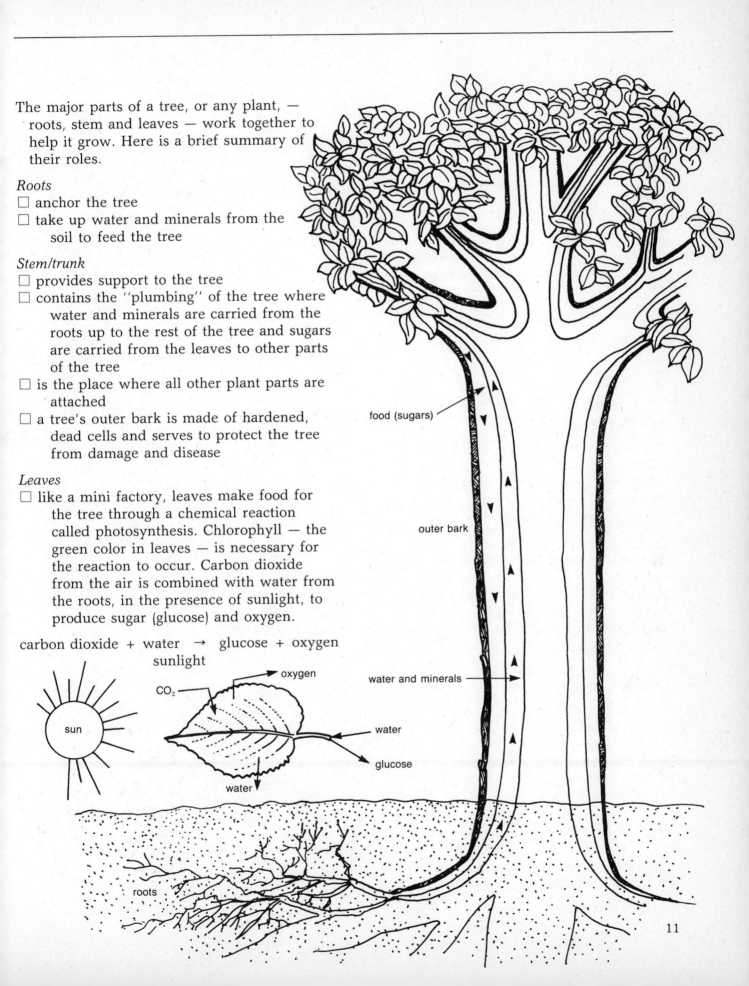

11

LESSON 1

Make A Tree Model

There are five major layers of cells within a tree. To explain the structure of a tree, you may use the cross-section of a tree given on Student Activity Sheet #1, "The Layers of a Tree", with the following details.

1. *Heartwood*
   This represents the oldest part of the tree. Most of the wood in the trunk of an old tree is heartwood. The cells are dead and serve to support the tree. Sometimes the heartwood can rot away or be eaten out by animals. This forms large hollows in the tree, creating excellent habitat for a variety of creatures such as flying squirrels, raccoons, and wood ducks.

2. *Sapwood or Xylem (pronounced zylem)*
   Surrounding the heartwood is a layer of sapwood or xylem consisting of straw-like tubes used to transport water and minerals from the roots to the rest of the tree. As the sapwood ages, it usually gets filled with resin-like material and dies, forming part of the heartwood. New xylem cells are produced by the cambium layer.

3. *Cambium*
   Next to the xylem is a very thin layer of cells called the cambium. It is this layer that produces all the new cells in the trunk, making it grow thicker each year (palm trees are an exception). On the inner side of the cambium, new xylem cells are produced. On the outer side of the cambium, new phloem cells are produced.

4. *Phloem (pronounced floam) or Inner Bark*
   The phloem cells consist of a series of straw-like tubes used to transport sap (containing the glucose produced in the leaves during photosynthesis) from the leaves to feed the rest of the tree. It also carries sugars stored in the roots to the rest of the tree in spring when the tree is starting to grow again. It is this flow that is tapped in sugar maples to make syrup.

5. *Bark*
   The outside layer on a tree is its bark. Different trees have different colors, textures, and thicknesses of bark but it all serves to protect the tree from disease and damage. The bark is made of dead phloem cells that are pushed farther away from the cambium layers as new phloem cells are produced. As the tree pushes outward, the bark often splits and peels under the pressure.

Activity

Students can make a model of a tree trunk using five pieces of contrasting colored plasticine. Students roll one color into a fat finger shape (this represents the heartwood). A second color is formed into a flat piece of medium thickness and then is wrapped around the first (this represents the xylem). A very thin layer is formed from a third color and wrapped around (this represents the cambium). The fourth color is formed into a piece of medium thickness and wrapped around (this represents the phloem). The fifth color should be left fairly thick and again wrapped (this represents the bark).

12

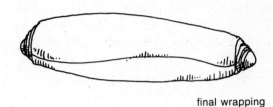

final wrapping

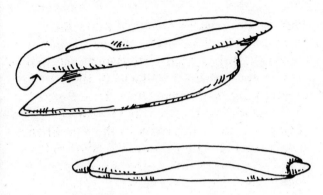

first and second colors

Have the students cut a slice from the middle of their models, and put it on their desks so they can see the layers of colored plasticine.

Using Student Activity Sheet #1, ask students to draw their slices in the space provided, number the layers, and then write the name of each layer. Have students write a few details about each layer beside the cross-section of the tree.

You may ask these follow-up questions after the drawing and writing have been done:

— which layer is the thickest? what is its role in the tree?
— which layer is the thinnest? what does it do?
— what might happen to a tree if its bark is peeled? why?

LESSON 2

Two Types of Trees

There are basically two types of trees — broad-leaf and needle-like. Trees such as maple, oak, and ash are broad-leafed; in most cases, broad-leaf trees are deciduous which means that they lose all their leaves at one time every year. Needle-like or scale-like leaf trees tend to be evergreen, keeping their leaves for two or more years, and shedding only a few at a time. They also tend to be coniferous, meaning that they produce cones instead of flowers. Examples are pine, spruce, and fir.

Activities

1. Using Student Activity Sheet #2, "Two Types of Trees," have students identify the parts of the maple and pine trees; the appropriate words have been given. The trees can be colored. Then ask the students the following questions:

— Describe the differences between the two trees. (maple has broad leaves and pine has needle-like leaves; maple has flowers and pine has cones; the shape of their silhouettes is different).

— What is the root word of coniferous and what do all coniferous trees have in common? (the root word is cone and all coniferous trees have cones).
— The maple tree loses all its leaves once every year which makes it a deciduous tree; in what season does it lose its leaves? (in the autumn). Why is autumn sometimes called the fall? (It is the season when the leaves fall off some trees.)

2. Take the students to an area where there is a variety of trees such as a park, school yard, conservation area, or woodlot. Have students stand beside a deciduous tree; a coniferous tree. As their knowledge of trees broadens, you can ask them to stand beside a tooth-edged deciduous tree.

LESSON 3

Looking At Leaf Shapes

The leaves of broad-leaf trees come in a great variety of shapes and forms. Students can learn about the differences by looking at and playing with the different shapes.

Activities

1. Give each student a copy of Student Activity Sheet #3 and Student Activity Sheet #3(a) "Looking at Leaf Shapes". Have the students cut out the leaves and glue them on the tree. The completed tree will be quite special as other trees always have leaves with the same shapes. Either use Student Activity Sheet #3(b) yourself or give copies to the class. Use these individual leaves to match up with the pasted down leaves. Have the students describe the shape and characteristics of each leaf. Write down names given to the shapes and identify the tree to which each leaf really belongs.

Possible shape names	Tree
smooth edge	— cucumber tree
toothed edge	— birch
oval	— beech
narrow	— black willow
triangular	— poplar
lobed	— sugar maple
compound	— sumac

2. Have students collect as many differently shaped leaves as they can, and bring them into the classroom. A large tree trunk and branches can be cut from construction paper and hung on a wall. The various leaves can be taped onto the tree to provide a display of different leaf shapes. In order to keep the leaves from drying out, they can be waxed by placing each leaf between a folded piece of waxed paper (waxed surface on inside), placing a cloth on top, and ironing with a hot iron until the wax melts and coats the leaf's surfaces.

3. Every community has trees that are characteristic of that area of land. You may use the following drawings of leaves, sometimes accompanied by their fruit or flower, to help the students identify the leaves they have collected. You can then determine which tree species are most common in your community and thus, in which type of vegetation zone you live. Are most of the leaves from deciduous trees? Are there both deciduous and coniferous? Do you have mostly conifers?

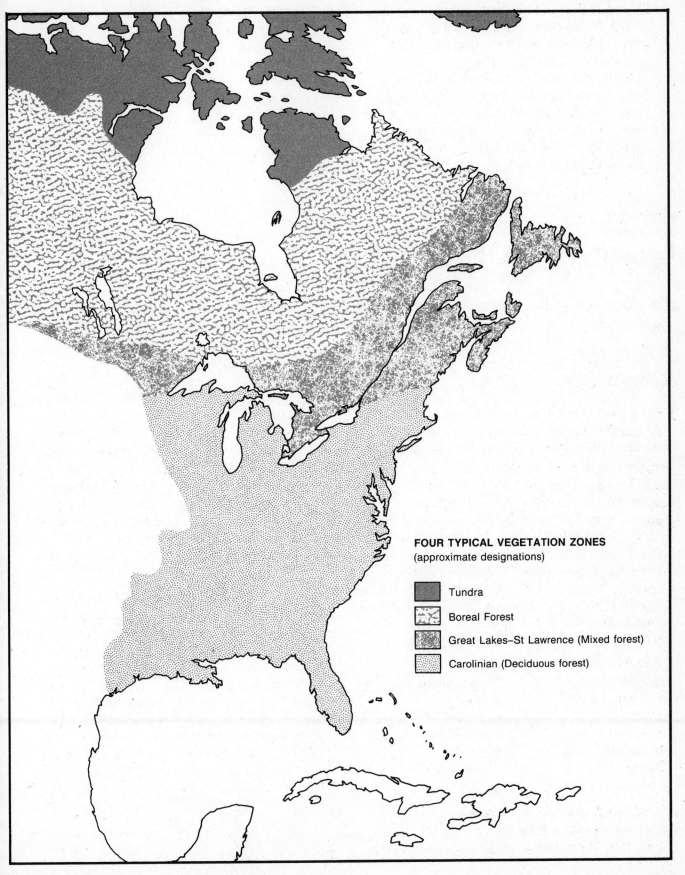

FOUR TYPICAL VEGETATION ZONES
(approximate designations)

- Tundra
- Boreal Forest
- Great Lakes–St Lawrence (Mixed forest)
- Carolinian (Deciduous forest)

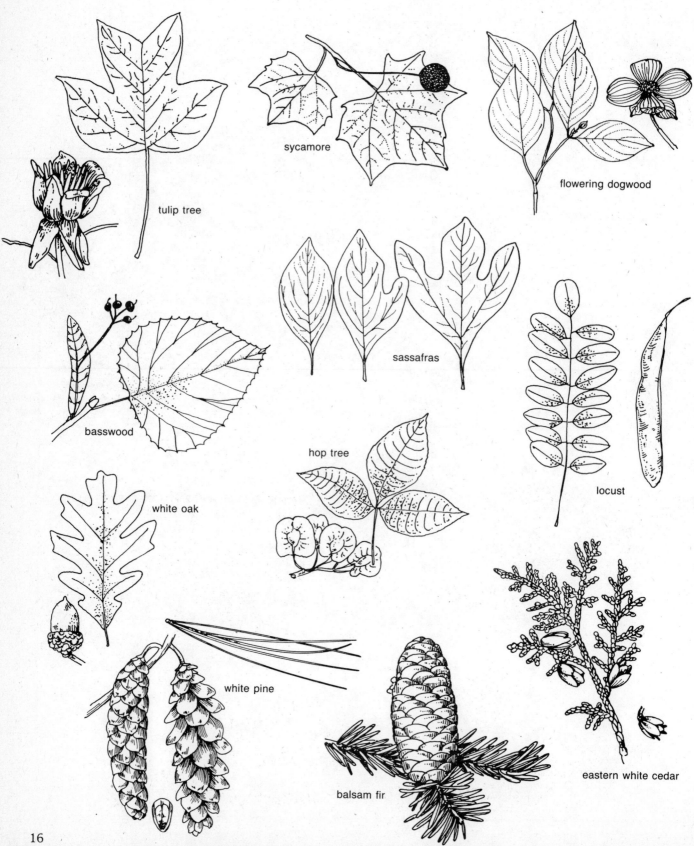

tulip tree

sycamore

flowering dogwood

sassafras

basswood

hop tree

locust

white oak

white pine

balsam fir

eastern white cedar

16

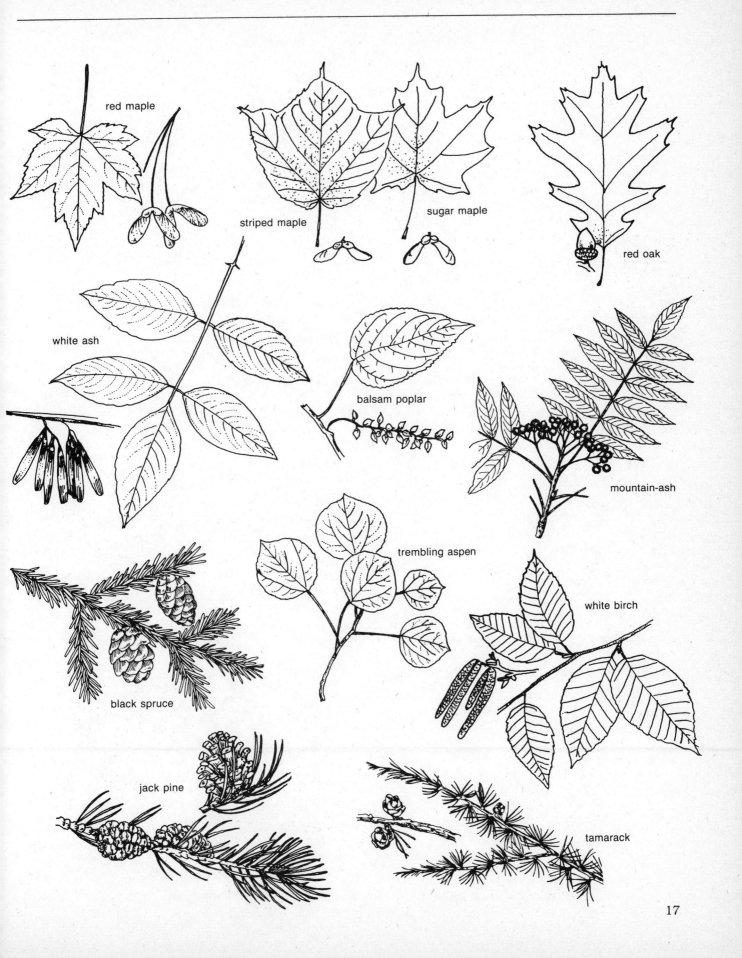

red maple

striped maple

sugar maple

red oak

white ash

balsam poplar

mountain-ash

trembling aspen

white birch

black spruce

jack pine

tamarack

LESSON 4

Conifers — Up Close

Trees such as pine, spruce, and fir are called conifers because they bear cones. Ripe cones are most easily found in the fall after they have dropped from the trees. By this time, they are brown and their scales have opened. The cones are the part of the tree where the seeds are found. The hard scales of the cone protect the seeds until the cone ripens, opens its scales, and releases the seeds to the wind. If you want to continue with a discussion on how cones are pollinated and their seeds dispersed, see Chapter Three.

The following activity gives students a chance to take some cones apart and see how they are "built".

Activity

You will need several large, ripe cones for each student (white pine or Norway spruce cones are good); heavy paper, glue, scraps of yellow and black felt, scissors.

— Have students separate the scales of their cones by gently pulling them away from the central stalk. There may be a dark-colored imprint on the top side of the scales where the seeds used to be attached.

— On the paper, have the students glue a 13 cm (about 5") wide ring of scales, flattest side down. A second ring of scales is then glued down just inside and overlapping the first ring. The paper should not show between the rings.

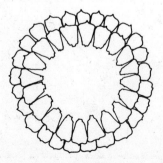

— The scales are glued down in decreasing rings until the inside of the circle is covered.

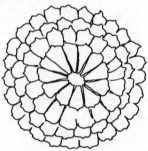

— To make the eyes, cut two rounds from yellow felt and two smaller rounds from black felt. Glue the black felt onto the yellow. Glue the eyes onto the conehead. A small triangle can be cut for a beak.

— Students may make coneheads of different animals.

— Students can write a story about their coneheads, giving them names, assigning a habitat, life span, eating habits, and special adaptations. Only their imaginations will limit the story content.

18

Protective Devices

Ask your students what trees need in order to survive. In general, all trees need water and minerals from the soil, and sunlight in order to grow. Having these things, though, doesn't guarantee success. Like most things in nature, trees have to protect themselves against enemies. What enemies do trees have? The list includes people, fire, disease, insects, other wildlife, other plants, high winds and lightning. This lesson will look at some of the ways trees protect themselves: (1) bark; (2) thorns; (3) toxins; (4) special characteristics.

Bark
Bark is like a tree's suit of armor. Its main purpose is to protect the tree from damage, especially from insect pests and diseases. Hard, thick bark is very difficult to penetrate so most insects, bacteria and fungi attack the wood of a tree that has holes already made in the bark. These holes may have been made by wildlife (such as woodpeckers), natural phenomena (such as a branch being snapped off in high winds) or people. Remind students that carving initials in tree bark or otherwise damaging the tree's suit of armor provides an open door to danger.

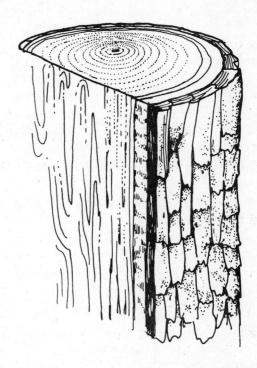

Different trees vary in the thickness of their bark. For instance, a birch tree may have only 6 mm of protection (about ¼''), whereas a Giant Sequoia from the west coast can have bark up to 60 cm thick (about 2')! In fact, the bark of the Giant Sequoia is so thick that it can actually protect the tree from fire.

Activity

Have students design a sign to teach others why a tree's bark is important and why people shouldn't damage it. Display the signs around the school, at an outdoor education centre or local park and conservation authority visitor centres.

Thorns
Ask your students if they climb trees. Which trees do they like to climb and which ones do they avoid? Chances are that trees with large thorns, such as hawthorns and locusts are low on the list of climbing favorites. Thorns provide a natural sort of barbed wire to keep wildlife and people from climbing up or moving in and damaging the tree. They may also keep wildlife from landing on the tree to eat its fruit.

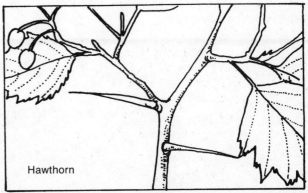

Hawthorn

Toxins

Since trees need water and minerals from the soil in order to grow, just like most other plants, they must compete with their neighboring plants for food. Some trees have developed "chemical weapons" to ensure that they will get the lion's share of the available resources. The roots of black walnut trees, for instance, secrete a toxin into the soil around the tree, killing off most existing vegetation and preventing other plants from growing near the tree. By reducing or eliminating the competition, the walnut tree keeps more of the water and minerals for itself.

Special Characteristics

Find out if any of your students have ever seen the aftermath of a forest fire. Ask them to describe it. At first the scene appears lifeless with fallen trees, charred stumps and blackened ground everywhere. Over the years, however, small plants such as grasses and wildflowers grow up, shrubs and tree seedlings grow and eventually a new forest is created. Although most trees are defenseless against a raging forest fire, some are especially adapted to ensure that their seeds will be around to grow after the fire is over. Jack pine trees have special cones that are tightly sealed with glue-like resins, protecting the seeds inside. These cones only open when they are exposed to the high temperatures caused by a fire. The fire melts away the resin and releases the seeds. After the forest has been burned down, the jack pine seeds are ready to start growing immediately in the nutrient-rich ash left by the fire. They can get a head start on almost all other plants and grow with very little competition.

Activity

You may use some closed jack pine cones for a teacher demonstration of what happens to the cones when they are heated.

Pass some closed cones around the room so students can see how tightly closed (almost sealed) the cones are.

Heat some cones on a hot plate. Ask students to predict what will happen. When the cones open, shake out the seeds to show students. Pass the open cones around the room for viewing.

Students can make their own drawings of what happens to jack pine seeds.

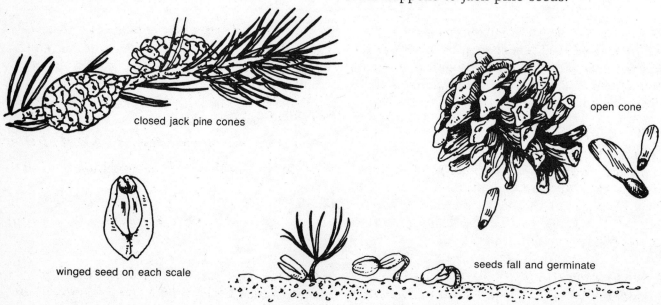

closed jack pine cones

winged seed on each scale

open cone

seeds fall and germinate

Name The Trees

Students should be introduced to the names of some of the more common trees they will be able to see. The names can be used as new vocabulary in spelling lessons or story writing.

Activities

1. Using Student Activity Sheet #4, "Tree Teaser", have students fill in the missing letters of tree names. (The answers are maple / oak / pine / birch / willow / cedar / spruce / tamarack) The names are shown in a "word forest" on the Activity Sheet.

2. Shape codes have been given to letters of the alphabet on Student Activity Sheet #5, "Tree Teaser". Students can use the shape code to figure out the names of trees; the first one has been done. (The answers are elm / beech / walnut / poplar / ash / chestnut / alder / hawthorn / maple / hemlock)

3. The little brain-teaser on Student Activity Sheet #6, "Tree Teaser" will have students thinking more about the names of different trees, and is also an opportunity to introduce a rhyming and spelling lesson. (The answers are ash / birch / elm / willow / maple / fir / beech / pine / yew / cherry / elder / oak)

4. Check your school library for books and videos that relate to trees. The titles can be factual or fictional. Ask students to bring in their favorite tree book from home. Set up a learning centre where the titles can be displayed. Read some of the books to the class during the year, and watch some films or videos.

Fact Sheets

At the end of the Student Activity Sheets are ten illustrated tree fact sheets, designed for student use. The fact sheets cover fairly common broad-leaf deciduous trees and coniferous trees. Each sheet has the following headings:

Name

Look At Me: a brief description of the tree, including shape, bark, buds, cones or flowers, fruit (if any), and leaves

Size: height of tree and diameter of trunk at maturity

Find Me: habitat and growing area

I'm Special: special features, adaptations, uses of wood

P.S.: other interesting details, related species

Words To Learn: important vocabulary

Activities

1. Whenever projects are assigned, encourage students to use the fact sheets. Each student can have a set and/or one set can be laminated and kept at the resource centre.

2. Divide the class into ten working groups, and assign each group a tree fact sheet. Ask each group to do the following:
   — locate the tree's range on a local map

— determine whether the tree is deciduous or coniferous
— name one animal species that depends on the tree for food or shelter
— research one of the related species listed under P.S.
— look up and explain the definitions for each of the words listed under Words To Learn
— collect magazine or catalogue pictures to make a collage of products manufactured from the wood of the tree

— research the uses of the tree by native people and/or early settlers.

3. Ask each group of students to research a species of tree not covered by the fact sheets. The research should be completed in the same format as the fact sheets. Once the research projects have been checked, the new fact sheets can be added to each collection, and used for future research projects.

CHAPTER TWO

The Big Picture

Trees come in a great variety of shapes and sizes, from nearly horizontally growing dwarfed spruce on the edge of the tundra to towering redwoods on the west coast that can be as tall as a 28 storey building. Trees are found in a wide variety of habitats, including jungles, rainforests, swamps, lowlands and uplands, cities and countrysides. Wherever trees grow, they play very important roles in the success of the ecosystem.

Some of their major contributions include:

(1) food and shelter for animals, other plants, and fungi
(2) water recycling
(3) erosion control
(4) air improvement

Dwarf spruce   Trembling aspen   Sugar maple   Redwood

LESSON 8

Be A Tree Detective

Trees provide food and shelter to a host of plant, fungi, and animal species. A partial list of animals may include woodpeckers, screech owls, wood ducks, many different songbirds, flying squirrels, raccoons, squirrels, porcupines, beavers, a huge variety of insects and other invertebrates, mice, bats, tree frogs, and some snakes. Trees are also hosts to lichens, moss, fungi, vines, ivies, and epiphytes (plants that germinate and root up in a tree instead of in the ground).

Activity

Give students a copy of Student Activity Sheet #7, "Trees Provide Food and Shelter" and ask them to look carefully for clues left by any kind of animals, including birds, insects, mammals. Students should be able to find ten clues, and circle them. Ask them to identify the ten animals that left the clues.

Answers

1. beaver dam or lodge
2. bird's nest in tree
3. woodpecker holes
4. squirrel's nest
5. bear claw marks on beech trunk
6. remains of red squirrel's lunch of pine cones
7. chrysalis on tree branch
8. leaves partially eaten (moth larvae)
9. branches nipped off by deer
10. bark chewed off base of young tree by mouse

LESSON 9

Where's The Water?

Trees are a very important part of nature's water cycle. They recycle water. Trees drink up huge amounts of water while they are growing in spring and summer. In fact, a large broad-leaf tree may soak up 4000 L (about 900 gallons) of water every day when it's hot and sunny. Most of the water is not stored in the tree but is used during photosynthesis and released through tiny openings in the leaves called stomata. This process is called transpiration. Droplets of water formed on the leaves are evaporated by the sun.

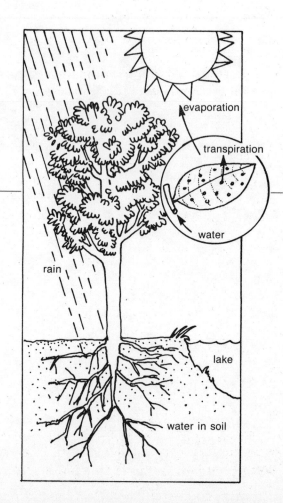

24

Activity

You can show students how water travels through a plant with this simple demonstration.

Tie a plastic bag securely around one leaf or a small cluster of leaves on a potted plant. Make sure you don't damage the stem when you secure the twist tie around the bag. Place the plant in a sunny location and water it thoroughly. Ask students to predict what will happen. At the end of the day, check the bag for water droplets transpired by the leaves. Have students explain what happened. How might a whole forest affect the local climate? If all the trees in a large area were cut down, how might that affect local climate?

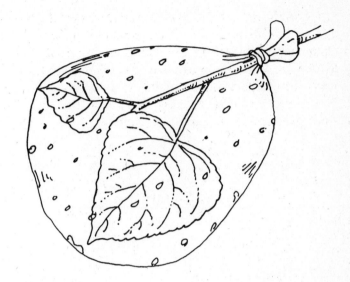

It's raining, it's pouring . . .

Trees play a major role in controlling erosion. The roots of trees help to bind soil particles together and stop them from being washed away by rain or blown away by erosion. The tree itself may also help prevent erosion by blocking surface winds and providing an umbrella-like canopy to reduce splash erosion and surface run-off.

Activity

You can simulate a tree's role in soil erosion with some simple equipment. This activity can be a teacher demonstration or several groups of students can do the simulation.

Fill a rectangular cardboard box with soil to just below the top. Separate the box, exactly in half, widthwise, by wedging a strip of cardboard into the soil as a divider. On one of the long sides of the box, cut holes at the top edge of the soil and a small distance in from the ends. The holes should be just big enough to fit a piece of plastic tubing. Insert tubing into holes. In one half of the box, plant several small upright plants such as geranium cuttings. Their "crowns" should be almost touching just as trees in the forest touch each other. The other half of the box is left as is. Prop up the

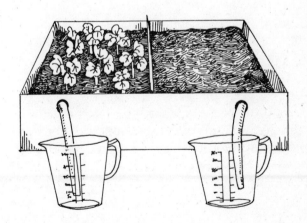

box on one side. Place the free end of each piece of tubing in a measuring cup. The measuring cups should be at a level lower than the box. Hold a watering can some distance above the box and water both halves equally.

25

Given that the plants represent trees or plant cover and the water represents rain, discuss with the students some of their observations.

Describe the water in the measuring cups. (The water in the cup below the bare soil should be dirtier because there was nothing to stop the rain from carrying away the soil.)

Which cup has less water? Why? (the cup below the planted soil should have less water in it because some of the rain would have been trapped by the plants.)

Describe the soil surface on each half of the box. (The bare soil should have pits and ridges where soil was eroded away by the rain.)

This experiment should show that vegetation, including trees, helps stop rain from washing away soil and also traps some of the water which can then be used for growth.

Trees At Work

Trees also improve the air. Leaves undergo photosynthesis in order to produce sugars (glucose) to feed the rest of the tree and help it to grow. There are two other consequences of the process of photosynthesis that are of direct benefit to people — and the air they breathe.

One of the ingredients in photosynthesis is carbon dioxide (CO_2). Leaves absorb vast amounts of CO_2 from the atmosphere during their daily lives. Due to air pollution from industry and automobiles, there is much more CO_2 in the air than there used to be naturally. This gas acts as a sort of shield in the sky, trapping the sun's heat close to the earth and not allowing it to escape back into the atmosphere. This is called the greenhouse effect. Warmer temperatures could have a disastrous effect on native plants and animals, water levels and climate. Since leaves can reduce the amount of CO_2 in the air, they are helping to reduce the greenhouse effect. One of the products of photosynthesis, along with glucose, is oxygen. The leaves release large amounts of oxygen back into the air every day. Since all animals, including people, need oxygen to breathe, the leaves are helping us.

Activity

To highlight the four important contributions that trees make to the ecosystem, have the students work on Student Activity Sheet #8, "Trees At Work", initially on their own and then as a class.

26

CHAPTER THREE

Multiplying and Dividing

Most trees that are planted along town or city streets and in backyards are already two or more years old and come from garden centres or nurseries. Ask your students where new trees come from originally. Most trees are started from seeds. If possible, take your class on a hike to a woodlot and find some seedlings. An alternative would be to bring potted seedlings into the class. These can be purchased at a nursery or dug up, with permission, in the wild (and safely returned after the lesson). Show the students an example or picture of what the seedlings will grow into. This chapter looks at how trees reproduce, disperse their seeds, and go through their life cycle.

The two main ingredients needed to make a seed are a pollen grain (male cell) and an egg (female cell). Pollen is formed on the male cones of conifers and on the anthers of the flowers of deciduous trees. The eggs are found inside the ovules on the scales of female cones or at the base of the pistil in flowers. How does the pollen get to the egg? Pollen can be carried to the female parts by wind, insects, birds, bats, other animals, or gravity.

When a tree seed is formed it contains a tiny embryo that will eventually grow into the roots, shoot, and leaves of the tree seedling. It also contains a tiny food supply to give the embryo the energy to grow once it germinates, or sprouts.

Activity

Review Student Activity Sheet #9, "Making Seeds" with the students to show visually how seeds are made on conifers and on deciduous trees.

LESSON 12

Sorting Seeds

Tree seeds come in all shapes and sizes. Ask students to describe any tree seeds they have seen. Bring in a selection of seeds to illustrate the variety; samples could be some of the following that are illustrated:

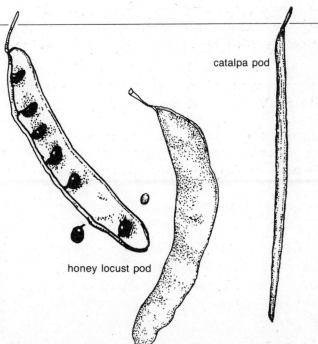

catalpa pod

honey locust pod

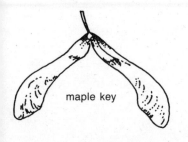

maple key

ash

elm

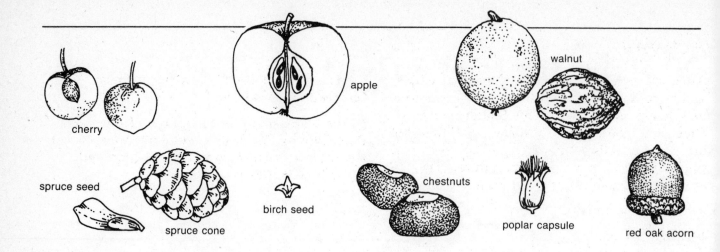

cherry

apple

walnut

spruce seed

spruce cone

birch seed

chestnuts

poplar capsule

red oak acorn

Activity

Using assorted seeds, nuts, and fruit and a nutcracker or knife, open the nuts, pods, or fruit to see the actual seeds inside.
Have students guess how each type of seed might be dispersed based on its physical appearance.

Divide the class into groups and give each group an assortment of seeds. Have each group develop its own classification system for its seeds. Have each group present the classification system to the rest of the class. Everyone can discuss the different ways in which seeds can be grouped, e.g. by size, shape, color, mass, method of dispersal.

LESSON 13

Seeds on the Move

If a tree's seeds all tried to grow right around the parent tree there would be too much competition for the available resources. In addition, many seedlings need a lot of sunlight to grow and wouldn't survive in the shade of the parent tree. For these reasons, trees need to disperse their seeds as far as possible in order to increase their chances of success. Dispersal alone, however, is not enough. The seed must also land in a spot with suitable soil, water, temperature and light conditions. How can a seed control where it will land? It can't. It's sheer luck when a seed finds a good home.

There are several ways for a tree's seeds to "move away from the parents' home". These include wind, water, and animals. Most conifers rely on wind to carry the small, light-weight seeds to a suitable spot for growth.

Some deciduous trees also take advantage of the wind by producing "winged" seeds to ride the wind. Examples include maple keys and elm seeds. Trees growing along water may drop their seeds in the water. The water carries the seeds along until they are deposited on another shore. If they land in a suitable spot, they can germinate and begin to grow. Coconuts and mangroves can actually travel unharmed in the oceans for a long time until they are deposited on a sandy shore somewhere. Animals are terrific seed carriers. Some, like birds, spread seeds by eating fruit and then leaving the undigested seeds in their wastes, often far from the original tree. Squirrels are well known for their habits of gathering nuts and storing them or burying them in new sites. It is likely that squirrels are responsible for planting a great many trees each year.

28

Activity

After talking about the various ways in which seeds are dispersed from their parent tree to a new home, give the students Student Activity Sheet #10, "Seeds on the Move". Ask them to draw a connecting line between each seed and the way in which it travels in nature. (The answers are maple key — wind; pine cone seed — wind; coconut — waves; cherries — bird; walnut — squirrel).

In the blank space at the bottom of the Student Activity Sheet, have students draw one of the seeds from their group's collection and show how it travels.

Get Growing

Once a seed lands in a suitable spot it can prepare for germination. Some seeds need to undergo a freeze (winter season) before they germinate, but others can sprout right away. Germination begins when the seed takes on water from the ground. The embryo absorbs the water and grows bigger and bigger until it bursts out of the seed coat (outer covering of the seed). The first part to appear is the root. It moves into the soil, grows tiny root hairs and begins to take up water and minerals from the soil to help the rest of the plant to get growing. The shoot pushes out of the seed next, expanding quickly until it breaks through the soil surface. Once the first leaves appear the seedling can begin photosynthesis and make its own food.

During spring and summer, trees in temperate climates are actively growing. Their trunks get thicker each year and their branches grow longer from the growth zones at their tips. The trees also prepare for their next year's growth by forming buds. The terminal buds (at the ends of branches) consist of hard, weather-proof bud scales that protect the tiny shoot inside. Buds along the sides of branches contain tiny leaves.

During winter, the water in the soil freezes and is not available to trees so they cannot continue to grow. When winter approaches deciduous trees, such as maples and oaks, drop their leaves, the tree stops photosynthesizing and becomes dormant until spring thaw. Although most conifers such as pines and spruces don't drop their leaves, they are also dormant in winter.

In spring, when the soil thaws and water is available again, the buds burst and the cells expand and grow into new branches and leaves. Eventually the tree will grow cones (conifers) or flowers (most deciduous trees) and produce seeds to complete the life cycle.

It is possible to grow some trees without seeds. Suckers are shoots that sprout from the roots of parent trees. The result is often a cluster of small trees, such as sumacs or aspen. Sometimes live branches that have fallen to the ground, or bent over until their tips touch the ground, can grow roots and start a new tree. This is called layering. Black spruce is such a tree if growing in a mossy environment. In addition, new trees can sprout from abandoned stumps.

Activities

1. You can show students how to germinate seeds, and then encourage them to grow their own trees from seeds. Local tree seeds need to overwinter before germination can occur but they could be collected in spring and used in this activity.

In Part A of this activity, a tree is grown from an avocado; Part B uses seeds from various citrus fruits. In all cases, students should be assigned responsibilities for observing and caring for the seeds and plants.

Part A:
You will need two avocado pits (in case one doesn't germinate), toothpicks, two glass jars and water, two plant pots and potting soil.

Hold the avocado pit in the mouth of the jar with the larger end downward. Place tooth-picks in the pit so that they rest on the edge of the jar and hold the pit there. The bottom of the pit should be in water.

Place the jar in a window. Keep the water level high. In a few weeks, the pit should split and a root emerge from the bottom. Shortly afterwards, a shoot (stem) will begin to grow upwards from the pit. When the plant sprouts its first leaves, remove the toothpicks, and carefully transfer the pit to a pot containing soil. Be very careful not to disturb the root. Place the pot in a sunny window.

Students can measure the growth of the root (until planted) and the stem on a daily or weekly basis, and chart the plant's growth.

Primary students could use a calendar and draw a picture to indicate growth patterns and changes on the days they occur. Junior students could use illustrations as well as linear measurements. This data could be transferred later to a variety of graphs, and integrated into the math curriculum.

Part B:
You will need seeds from grapefruit, oranges, lemons, or limes that have been soaked in water overnight, paper towels or rags, a glass jar and water, plant pots and potting soil.

Line the sides of a glass jar with soaking wet paper towels or rags. Slide some seeds between the towels and the side of the jar so that the seeds are easily visible.

Keep the towels/rags wet, and watch the seeds for signs of germination over the next 10 days. Seeds will germinate more quickly if the seed coat has been removed with a blade or sandpaper.

Once the seeds germinate, carefully plant them in pots and place in a sunny window. Each student could plant a seed in a small peat cup that has had drainage holes punched in the bottom.

2. To show students how roots can grow from a branch to start a new plant, have them take cuttings from a geranium plant. The cuttings can be planted in peat pots. Although geraniums are not trees, they are easy to root and will demonstrate the concept of rooting.

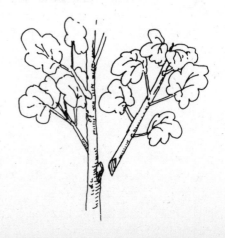

At the same time as students are rooting their cuttings, place some other geranium cuttings and young willow branches in jars of water. Replace the water every three days. This will allow students to see what is happening below ground level with their potted cuttings.

Cut a few drainage holes in the bottom of the pots. Carefully cut a 15 cm (about 6″) shoot from a geranium plant, near a joint where a leaf meets the stem. Pull off the lowest couple of leaves. Plant the cutting in potting soil so that about half the cutting is buried. Water the soil, and place a plastic bag over the pot and cutting. Tie the bag shut.

Leave the plant in a shaded spot for two to three weeks. To check whether the roots have grown, gently tug on the stem; if the cutting doesn't slip out easily, then it has rooted.

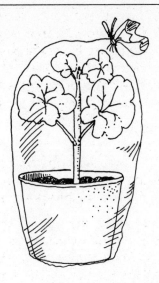

When the cutting has rooted, remove the plastic bag and keep the plant in the shade until it begins to grow well. Transfer the plant to a sunny location.

CHAPTER FOUR

Winter Is Coming

Autumn is a terrific time to take your students outside to look at the changing colors of the trees. Some of the following lessons combine a hike with a specific activity, and teach the students how different trees prepare for the winter. This chapter discusses how both deciduous and coniferous trees face cold weather.

Activity

In September, when the leaves are still green, take the students outside to look at a variety of trees. Have each student choose one tree to be observed over the next nine months — an adopt-a-tree project. You may want to encourage students to adopt a deciduous tree, simply because there will be more changes. Conifers won't require as much work!

The students can observe and record information about their trees in a booklet or on a large piece of chart paper. On a monthly basis, at least, revisit the trees to note any changes. By the end of June, the students should have an overview of their trees throughout the seasons.

If appropriate, and you have the facilities, set up a data base on the computer, and enter the information on the various kinds of trees being observed by the students.

LESSON 15

Changing Colors and Falling Off

Ask your students what some of nature's signs of autumn are. The changing colors and dropping off of deciduous leaves are clear signs of colder weather. Why do leaves change color and fall? During winter the water in the soil is frozen, so it is unavailable to the trees. In order to stop water loss, the deciduous trees stop photosynthesizing (a process that requires a lot of water) and get rid of their leaves (a lot of water is lost through the leaves during transpiration). The color change is due to the breakdown of chlorophyll — the green pigment in the leaves. Although the yellows and oranges were always present in the leaves, until now they were masked by the chlorophyll. Once it goes, the other colors are visible. The brilliant reds are produced in some leaves, such as sugar maples, in the fall.

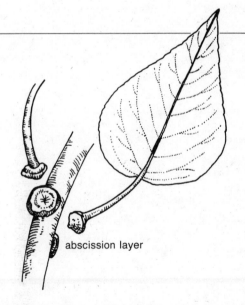

abscission layer

The tree cuts off the food and water supply to the leaves by growing a thin layer of tissue (the abscission layer) between the branch and the leaf's stem. Eventually the leaf can hold on no longer and is easily knocked off by wind or rain.

33

Activity

Arrange to take the students on a "rainbow" hike to allow them to really look at the multitude of colors produced by different leaves in the autumn. Such a hike will also provide an opportunity to discuss the ways in which trees prepare for winter. Obtain some paint chip samples from a hardware or paint store in yellows, reds, oranges, browns, rusts, and purples. Cut the paint chips into their separate colors and mix them up in an opaque bag.

Once you have reached an area where there is a variety of deciduous trees and shrubs whose leaves have changed color, have each student pull out an equal number of color chips from the bag. Explain that these are the colors they need to find on their hike. When students find their color on a leaf, they can call out and show it to others. Then, that color can be put in another container.

Back in the classroom, those chips that matched up with nature can be made into a collage to show the variety that occurs.

Next Year's Buds

Although this year's leaves are gone, next year's have already been formed and are hidden away behind hard, weatherproof bud scales along the branches. At the tips of the branches are terminal buds that protect next year's new shoots. Along the sides of the branches are smaller buds (lateral buds) that hide tiny leaves. In the spring when water is available again, the buds absorb water and swell until the scales split, releasing the new growth inside.

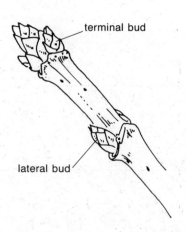

terminal bud

lateral bud

Activities

1. Once the leaves have fallen, buds are a good way to identify trees. If you can take a nature hike, the mini-guide to buds on Student Activity Sheet #11, "Mini-Guide to Buds" will help identify some of the buds you see.

2. If you, or someone you know, is pruning a tree or shrub in the fall, ask for the branches that are clipped. You will need branches that have terminal and lateral buds.

   Divide the class into groups according to the number of branches you have. Have each group identify the terminal and lateral buds. Ask them to identify the shape, feel, and smell of the buds. Each group can carefully peel away the bud scales to see what's inside and how the bud is constructed.

3. In late winter, buds can be forced to open early by cutting small branches, bringing them inside, and putting them in a jar of water. Pussy willows and forsythia are commonly forced branches. This will give the students a sneak preview of what will appear in spring.

34

Bark Examination

Bark is another good clue to tree identification in winter. Bark comes in all shapes and textures. Bark is made from dead phloem cells that are pushed farther and farther away from the inside of the tree as new phloem cells are produced. As the tree pushes outward, the bark often splits and peels under pressure, leaving some trees with loose bark in strips, scales, flakes, or deep grooves. Beech trees, on the other hand, have a more ''stretchable'' bark that remains smooth as the tree grows.

Activity

A hike can be conducted along a street where trees are growing, in a local park, or a wood-lot. The best area is one in which there are a few different types of trees, and preferably trees of different ages.

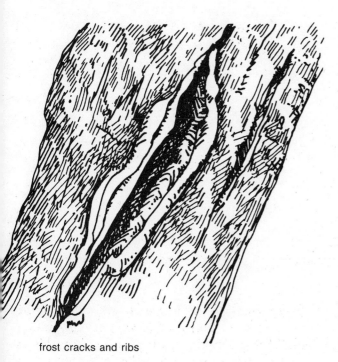

frost cracks and ribs

Give each student a piece of paper and a crayon. Have them do a bark rubbing by holding the paper against the bark and lightly coloring over the paper. The pattern of the bark will show through.

Ask the students to look at the bark, feel it, and smell it. They can record their descriptive words on the paper beside the bark rubbing.

Remind the students to look for signs of insects and other wildlife, plants such as moss, and frost cracks and ribs.

If you're in a wooded area on a very cold night, you may hear a loud bang, sounding like a gun shot. Chances are, what you've heard is a tree cracking. Frost cracks sometimes appear on trees because of a sudden drop in temperature, especially in spring or fall. The outside of the tree cools quickly and shrinks, but the inside stays warm and doesn't shrink. The resulting tension causes the outside to split. To heal the wound, the tree builds up scar tissue around the crack the next spring. Since this new tissue is usually weak, it tends to split again each winter. The result is the build up of a frost rib around the crack.

Conifers

Since conifers keep their same general appearance year-round, they are easier to identify in winter than some deciduous trees. Cones are a good clue to a conifer's identity as well as the overall shape of the tree, or its silhouette.

Activity

The silhouettes and cones of eight conifers have been provided on Student Activity Sheets #12 to #15, ''Conifers''. Copy and cut out these pictures and mount them on cardboard to make flashcards. The names of the conifers can be written on the back of the flashcards. (The answers are 1. white spruce; 2. black spruce; 3. white pine; 4. red pine; 5. eastern white cedar; 6. tamarack; 7. balsam fir; 8. jack pine)

Discuss tree shapes and cone shapes with the students. If possible, bring in a selection of cones for the students to view. Use the flashcards with the class, and then leave them in a learning centre area so that the students can practise their skills of recalling which conifer has which shape.

Remind students to look for tree silhouettes when they are on field trips; this can be done even from a moving school bus or car.

CHAPTER FIVE

Trees As Homes

It has been noted that one of the main contributions that trees make to the ecosystem is that of providing food and shelter to many plant, fungi, and animal species. The best way to learn about trees is to go out and look at them. Students can explore a tree with their hands and a magnifying glass.

LESSON 19

The Tree Creatures

There are insects that live on tree roots; insects that like living behind loose bark; insects that burrow into the bark; moss and lichens that grow on bark; and all kinds of creatures living in leaves.

Activity

Review Student Activity Sheets #16 and #17, "A Tree is our Home" that show some examples of those that make a tree their home. Armed with these pictures, a magnifying glass, and a trowel, take the students on a tree hike.

Explore your tree from the ground up. Use the trowel to dig gently around the base of the tree. You may see some of the tree's surface roots, and, if you are lucky, you'll uncover some root-feeding insects such as cicada nymphs. Loose bark near the base of the tree is also a good hiding place for spiders and cocoons.

Scan the cracks and crevices of the bark for insects and other invertebrates. Some spiders make tube-shaped webs on trees, while engraver beetles and carpenter ants leave entrance holes. Use the magnifying glass to look more closely.

Check for the tell-tale signs of woodpeckers and sapsuckers.

The bark may also be supporting other plants such as moss and lichen.

Look for knobby growths on leaves that are caused by insect galls or fungi. Tiny, transparent tunnels across a leaf are the sign of leaf miners. Unroll any cigar-shaped leaves to see if the young insects are still at home.

Are there any nests in the branches? You may find caches of food left by squirrels or birds in the crotches of large trees.

LESSON 20

Cavity Nesters

When you are outdoors in the woods, always keep an eye out for cavities in trees. These may be used for nesting or feeding. There is an amazing and often unseen community of cavity dwellers that is fascinating.

If you come across a cavity, take a peak inside if you can reach it. You may be surprised to find feathers, bones, scat, fur, or a number of other traces of animal life in the holes.

Cavity nesters include mammals such as squirrels, opossums, martens, weasels, and raccoons. Many different kinds of birds are considered to be cavity nesters. These include woodpeckers, wrens, titmice, warblers, chicka- dees, owls, bluebirds, wood ducks, sapsuckers, nuthatches, swallows, sparrows, swifts, kes- trels, buffleheads, and goldeneyes. Another group of cavity nesters are occasional visitors; wasps, bumblebees, gray tree frogs, and honey bees fit into this category.

Who makes the cavities? Most often, wood- peckers carve out nesting cavities in trees. Chickadees and nuthatches can also carve out their own homes. Some holes are caused by fungus decaying exposed wood.

Once the primary excavators have done all the work and used the holes for themselves, they may use their nest site again or abandon it. This leaves a vacant home for a secondary cavity nester, or free-loader.

Who decides who gets to move in? First-come, first-served is often the rule. Early returning migrants can get a head start and move in before the other neighbors arrive. If there is a line-up however, intimidation of the competi- tion is usually enough to stake a claim. Fight- ing is sometimes necessary. The small size of some birds can be an advantage, letting them fit where larger animals cannot.

Nesting cavities are vital to the survival of many species. They are important for nesting, resting, raising young, storing food, escaping predators, and sheltering from bad weather.

Activities

1. This game will familiarize students with different species of cavity dwellers and will also illustrate the difficulty they have in the wild to find a suitable nesting cavity.

   Copy three sets of Student Activity Sheets #18 to #22, ''Cavity Nesters'', each on a different color of paper. Cut out the sil- houettes of the cavity nesters on two sets.

   In a room, such as a gymnasium, where stu- dents can run around freely, tape up the individual circles from the third copy. Put some in obvious locations, others in more obscure locations. Place a round of sticky tape in the middle of each cavity nester.

   Divide the class into groups, and give them the cut-out silhouettes. Explain the rules of the game while still in the classroom.

   Each group of students represents a group of cavity nesters; each cavity nester must find a tree cavity in order to nest, repro- duce, and survive.

   The room where the circles are placed represents a forest with a variety of cavities

suitable for different species. However, there are only enough cavities for half of them. Students must match their silhouettes to those on the circles, once found, and they can be secured by the tape.

After the game, discuss with the students what will happen to those creatures that didn't find a cavity. They may move to another forest to look for a home; if they are able, they may create a new cavity in this forest; if they cannot find a suitable site, they won't be able to breed this year or they may die from exposure or predation.

Discuss with the students the fact that dead trees in a forest are important because they provide prime habitats for cavity nesters.

Discuss with the students how we can help conserve cavity nesting wildlife through leaving some dead trees standing in managed woodlots, through leaving some rotting logs and old stumps on the ground, through leaving some areas of forest uncut, and through building and erecting nest boxes.

2. Grey squirrels are cavity dwellers in large snag (dead) and den trees found in hardwood forests and woodlots or city parks and backyards with shrubby undergrowth. Besides living in tree dens, squirrels construct dreys, protective shelters made of leaves to provide escape and summer shelter. When more preferable tree cavities are lacking in winter, these dreys will be used for year-round protection.

Den boxes or squirrel nest boxes provide an alternative for squirrels when cavities are scarce. Den boxes should be positioned so that the entrance hole is not struck by the prevailing winds and so that the entrance hole is next to the tree trunk for easy access. To make the den box more attractive to squirrels, a layer of clean, dry leaves should be added to the bottom of the box, to a maximum of halfway up.

To make a squirrel nest box, you will need: wood that is 1.25 cm (½'') thick

— 1 backplate: 20 cm (8'') × 60 cm (24'')
— 1 front plate: 17.5 cm (7'') × 40 cm (15'')
— 1 roof: 20 cm (8'') × 25 cm (10'')

— 2 side plates: 20 cm (8'') × 42.5 cm (16'')
— 1 floor: 17.5 cm (7'') × 20 cm (8'')
2 lag screws, 2 nails, 1 hook & eye assembly, drill, hammer

Drill holes at the top and bottom of the backplate for lag screws.

In one sideplate, drill a hole 7.5 cm (3'') in diameter. Locate the bottom of the entrance 30 cm (11'') above the floor. In the other sideplate, drill at least two holes .6 cm (¼'') in diameter near the top to provide ventilation.

Cut .5 cm (¼'') off each corner of the floor to provide drainage.

Assemble the pieces as shown. Note that the roof is not centred over the box but that a lip extends out over the entrance hole to provide protection from the elements. The door is hinged with nails at the bottom and the hook and eye assembly is attached at the top and side.

Erect the nesting box at least 2 m (6') up in a tree.

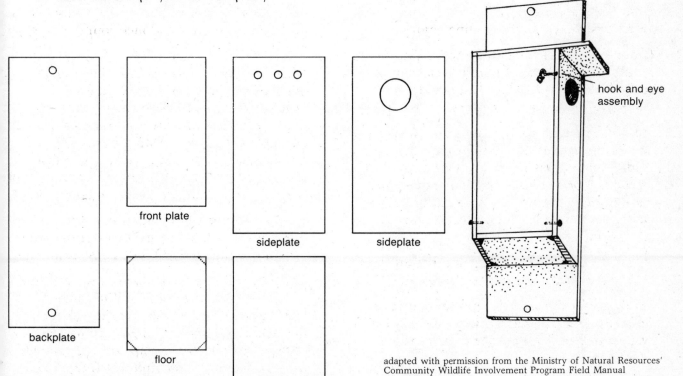

front plate

sideplate

sideplate

backplate

floor

roof

hook and eye assembly

adapted with permission from the Ministry of Natural Resources' Community Wildlife Involvement Program Field Manual

Aging The Home

In addition to checking for insect life, such as scale insects, or other animal life on branches, you can also discover something about the tree's growth rate over the past years by reading a twig. You can tell the age of a tree and what has happened to it through its growth cycle by reading a cross-section of a trunk.

Activities

1. By examining a twig, you can see where the leaves were attached, how much the tree grew in a year, and where next year's leaves will be. This is a great activity in the fall or winter after the leaves have dropped.

Find last year's growth rings, a ridge of lines around the twig. The distance from the growth rings to the bud at the top of the twig (terminal bud) measures the tree's growth during the year. There is a lot of variation among species.

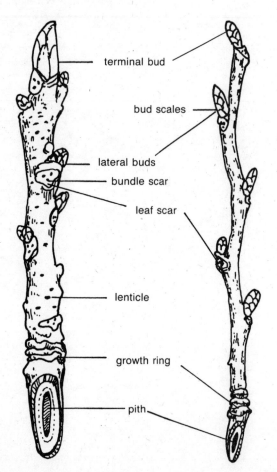

- terminal bud
- bud scales
- lateral buds
- bundle scar
- leaf scar
- lenticle
- growth ring
- pith

Look for the flat leaf scars along the twig. These scars are left when the leaves fall off. Inside each scar you can see tiny dots called bundle scars. These mark the place where the leaf's veins were connected to the tree's "plumbing" of xylem and phloem tubes. Also, on the twig's bark you may notice tiny dots or lines called lenticles. These allow air to flow into the cells of the tree.

The buds along the twig are covered tightly with bud scales to protect the hibernating leaf inside. The shape of the bud is an important clue for tree identification.

2. If you took a cross-section of a tree, you would see a series of light and dark rings. The light rings of wood represent the spring growth, while the thicker-walled, summer-wood shows up as a dark ring. Each pair of light and dark rings represents one year's growth. By counting the pairs of rings, you can determine the approximate age of a tree.

If possible, obtain a cross-section of a tree or a stump to bring into the class. Otherwise, this activity can be done outdoors, possibly in combination with another lesson in this chapter. It is easiest to see the rings on freshly-cut, wet wood.

Have the students determine the age of the tree by counting the sample's rings. If it is not possible to bring a sample into the classroom, or if you would like an extension activity, use Student Activity Sheet #23, "Age a Tree". (The answers are: 1. 11 years old; 2. best growth at 3 years, least growth at 9 years; 3. drought, pollution, insect damage could have hampered growth; 4. scar is caused by fire)

Discuss with the students whether the light and dark rings are the same width, and why not. Since the light rings represent spring growth which is usually more rapid and extensive, the light rings are wider than the dark, summer growth.

Discuss with the students why certain years produced wider rings than other years. Growing conditions do vary from year to year; a wider ring means better growing conditions.

Discuss with the students the factors that can affect the growth of a single tree, such as sunlight, rainfall, temperature, pollution, fire, disease, insect infestation, physical damage, decay, and competition with other trees.

3. It is possible to tell the age of a house by looking at the wood with which it was built. Core samples of beams and other wooden supports are taken and matched with a "tree ring map" of the same species of wood from the same general area. It is assumed that the house was built the same year the tree was cut. The following illustration shows how the outermost ring of the core sample is placed to coordinate with the tree ring map.

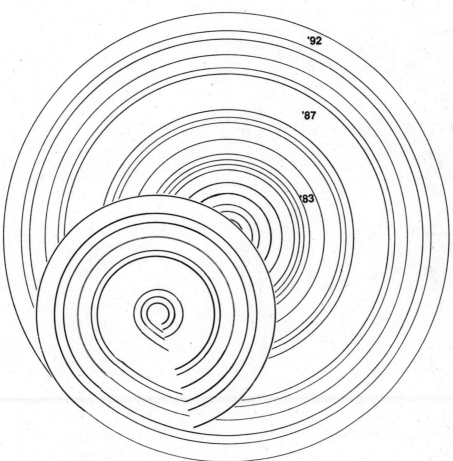

This tree was cut in 1992 and began life in 1984

CHAPTER SIX

Trees and People

From toothpicks to houses, trees provide society with an enormous array of products. This chapter will increase the students' awareness of how dependent we are upon trees and how the forestry industry operates. (For information on the importance of trees in nature see Chapter 2). Conservation has been stressed in preceding chapters and this chapter is no exception. Forestry is an accepted and vital industry in the North American economy and obviously provides society with many important products. However, just as we would not say that it is wrong to cut down any trees, we would also not agree that it is fine to cut down as many trees as industry deems necessary. There are good and bad forestry practices and we believe that there are forests where no trees should be cut for timber — such as unique old growth forests like Temagami in northern Ontario and Big Reed Pond Preserve which is north of Baxter State Park in Maine, and protected habitats such as parks and nature reserves. Areas that are cut must be worked in an environmentally sensitive way and regenerated successfully.

LESSON 22

Trees And Me

Tree products are an important part of our everyday life. Tree products include wood, paper, cardboard, cork, resin, paints, rubber, some food, and cellulose that is mixed with certain chemicals to make carpeting, fabrics, cellophane, photographic film, buttons, combs, pillows, upholstery, and even eye glass frames.

Activities

1. Using Student Activity Sheet #24, "Trees And Me", have the students fill in as much information on the classroom inventory as they can on their own. Record the information from all the students on a wall chart.

Discuss with the students the various tree products, other than wood, that they found in their inventory.

Discuss with the students what seemed to be the most common uses for trees in their classroom survey.

How many substitute materials for tree products did they find? Try to brainstorm some more substitutes.

Discuss with the students how our lives would be different if there were no more trees available to be cut. Although trees are considered a "renewable resource" because they can be replaced by growing new trees, it takes many years for a tree to grow big enough to be cut. Discuss with the students some ways in which we could lessen our need for tree products, and reduce or slow down the rate at which trees are cut.

Have the students take home the bedroom inventory, also on Student Activity Sheet #24. Did any new information come from the additional inventory? Add to the wall chart.

2. Trees not only provide us with shelter and warmth, but they also feed us. Have your students choose a food from the following list, and ask them to write a research project on that food. The following points should be covered in the project:

— from what part of the tree does the food come?
— in which countries does the tree grow naturally?
— can the tree be cultivated in other areas, and if so, where?
— how big does the tree grow?
— if the tree can be cultivated, how is this done?
— in what forms is the food available in a grocery store or market? (e.g. apples can be fresh, dried, in sauce, and pies)
— if the food needs to be processed before it is eaten, describe the processing
— list any interesting facts about the food that were discovered during research
— draw a picture of the food and the tree that produces it

— copy out a recipe that uses the food (include a note about the source of the recipe, e.g. book, magazine, family member)
— if possible, include a sample of the food

Students can present their projects to the class, and then they can be displayed in the school.

SUGGESTED LIST OF FOODS	
allspice	limes
almonds	maple sugar
apples	nectarines
apricots	nutmeg
cacao	olives
cherries	oranges
chestnuts	papayas
cinnamon	peaches
cloves	pears
coconuts	pecans
dates	pine nuts
figs	plums
grapefruit	tangerines
kumquats	walnuts
lemons	

LESSON 23

Forest Management

The best way to learn about forestry and forest management is to visit a managed forest and talk to a forest manager. Ideally, you should visit an unmanaged forest or woodlot the same day, for comparison.

The science of forestry is the study of the history of trees, how they grow, how long it takes for them to mature, and what problems can affect their growth. All this research is applied to the business of forestry, which cultivates, protects, and harvests trees, as well as reforests cut areas.

Forest management involves several aspects: wise care and harvesting of trees, growing certain trees under certain conditions (called silviculture), and protecting trees from forest fires, insects, and disease. In Canada, most of the forested land is publicly owned Crown land, and is managed by the individual provinces. The federal government is in charge of the forests of the Yukon and NWT. The provinces lease the Crown land to private companies who then harvest the trees according to provincial regulations. In the U.S.A., the U.S. Forest Service is a federal agency that looks after forest management.

Some forests have been planted as a farmer would plant a crop. These plantations are started from seed collected in the wild. The seedlings are grown in a tree nursery until they are large enough to be transplanted in the wild. The result is an area of even-aged trees of the same species — usually pine or spruce — quite unlike a natural forest that offers a

44

wider range of species and ages. Although plantations do offer some wildlife habitat, it is much less diverse than a natural habitat.

Most forested areas have been cut at least once. However, some areas were cut so long ago that their trees are now old. These types of forests are called old-growth forests and are extremely important for wildlife as well as being a vital part of our natural heritage. There is an ongoing debate between industry, government, environmentalists, and native peoples regarding the cutting of old-growth forests, such as Temagami in northern Ontario, Hafey Hardwood and Gero Island in Maine.

Activities

1. Arrange a visit to a managed and an unmanaged woodlot. If possible, have a staff person from your local forest management body come along as a guide. Discuss the basics of forestry and forest management with the class before the field trip. Have the students prepare a list of questions they wish to ask.

   Copy Student Activity Sheet #25, "A Tale of Two Forests" and review it with the students before the trip. The advantages and disadvantages of the two types of forest could be set up in the form of a panel discussion or debate after the visit.

2. Although forests provide nature and society with so many different benefits, people do not always agree on what is the best treatment or use of a forest. This activity allows your students to do some role playing to investigate the many sides of the land use debate over forests. The roles can be assigned or the roles can be copied, cut up and placed in a bag for students to draw at random. The roles are given on Student Activity Sheet #26, "Sharing the Land Roles". Each student who is to play a role (except the mediators) should take an assistant to help him/her prepare the "case". Allow as much time as you think is necessary for preparation. A team of four mediators will also be formed. It will be their duty to listen to the cases presented by the others and help reach a consensus. If there are extra students left in your class, create new roles, double up on assistants or have them take notes on the blackboard, jotting down the major points made by each presenter.

Presentations should last about five minutes each. The order of presentations can be determined at random or on a volunteer basis. At the end of everyone's presentation, each person will be allowed a one minute rebuttal or summary. The mediators will then summarize the arguments and try to reach some kind of compromise. (This may not be possible.)

Read the activity introduction to the students to set the scene for their role playing.

SPRINGHILL FOREST

Springhill Forest is a public forest near a small town. It is one of the few remaining uncut old-growth forests in the region. Some of the pine and maple trees growing here are the largest of their kind in the region and several species of rare plants also grow here. The area is full of wildlife, some rare and threatened and it is a favourite spot for naturalists to come bird-watching, hiking and camping. In the winter skiers and skidooers share the forest.

A local forestry company has recently applied to the government for a license to cut the trees in the forest for timber. Due to their size, many of the trees are extremely valuable and the work will create jobs for local people. Although not all the trees are mature, due to the difficulty of selectively cutting trees, they will be clearcut and then replanted afterwards with red pine for future harvest.

A town meeting has been called at which all people interested in the future of the forest may come and present their thoughts. What happens to the forest will be decided on the basis of the presentations.

After setting the scene, remind students that they should
— be brief and to the point
— state their facts clearly, and make sure they are accurate points
— be clear about what they want and about what might happen if they don't win

— offer possible alternatives to the proposal
— take notes during the presentations about what the other speakers say in order to use that information in their final one minute of presentation

Making Paper

Paper mills can produce up to 48 000 m of paper per hour (about 30 000 yards). Although you can't match that speed, you can have fun making paper with the class, and recycling at the same time. The students can help tear up the scrap paper, and once you have demonstrated the method, they can take turns screening the pulp and laying it out. You will need:

2 flat wooden picture frames, 12.5 × 17.5 cm (about 5 × 7")
nylon screening and a stapler
scrap paper (no plastic or staples)
plant and vegetable scraps
a bowl
a blender
water
a large plastic basin
1 sponge
2 clean dish towels and an iron

Stretch a piece of screening over one frame and staple it in place all around the edges. This frame is your mold.

Tear scrap paper into little bits, and soak pieces in a bowl of warm water for 30 minutes.

Place a handful of the wet scraps into the blender that is half full of warm water. Blend at medium speed until the pieces have been totally "mushed". Add some plant or vegetable scraps to the pulp and blend again. If you want colored paper, you may add a few drops of non-toxic fabric dye.

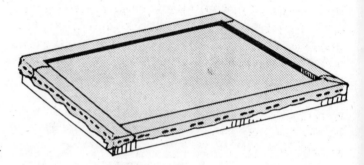

Pour the pulp into a large plastic basin, half full of warm water.

Lay the second frame on top of the mold. Holding both frames together, dip them into the basin and scoop up some of the mixture. The more pulp on the screen, the thicker the paper will be.

Jiggle the frames back and forth to even out the layer of pulp on the mold. The empty frame acts as a border to help make the edges of the paper more even. Once the water has drained through the screen, place the frames on a counter and carefully remove the empty frame.

Carefully lay the mold, pulp-side down, on a clean dish towel. Use the sponge to absorb any excess moisture from the back of the screen. Gently remove the screen so that just the paper is lying on the towel.

Quickly put another dish towel over the paper, and iron at medium, dry setting. When the towel feels dry, stretch it out at the sides to loosen the paper. Remove the towel and carefully peel off the paper.

Trees in Jeopardy

American chestnut

cucumber tree

Ask your students to imagine a forest with large trees and several deer. A woodcutter and a hunter enter the forest. How will the trees and the deer defend themselves from their respective enemies? The students will figure out that the deer have the opportunity to escape danger by running away and hiding but that the trees, like all plants, cannot move and are completely vulnerable to destruction. For instance, in Ontario there is one tree listed as endangered (cucumber tree), three listed as threatened (Kentucky coffee tree, American chestnut tree, blue ash), and three designated as rare (Shumard oak, hop tree, dwarf hackberry). General definitions of those terms are as follows:

Endangered Species: Any indigenous species of fauna or flora that, on the basis of the best available scientific evidence, is indicated to be threatened with immediate extinction throughout all or a significant portion of its range.

Threatened Species: Any indigenous species of fauna or flora that, on the basis of the best available scientific evidence, is indicated to be experiencing a definite non-cyclical decline throughout all or a major portion of its range, and that is likely to become an endangered species if the factors responsible for the decline continue unabated.

Rare Species: Any indigenous species of fauna or flora that is represented by small but relatively stable populations, and/or that occurs sporadically or in a very restricted area or at the fringe of its range, and that should be monitored periodically for evidence of a possible decline.

All of the designated tree species are found in the Carolinian or Deciduous Forest Zone (*see* map of forest zones in Chapter 1, Lesson 3). Because of their very limited natural distribution, these trees, like many other Carolinian species, are very vulnerable to population decline. Habitat loss is a major factor in this forest zone due to the large concentration of population, industry and recreation in the area. Some species, such as the cucumber tree, have also suffered from logging practices. In order to improve the net worth of a stand of trees, less valuable timber such as the cucumber tree has been selectively cast out in the past. Today it is protected under Ontario's Endangered Species Act. Other species are protected where they grow in national or provincial parks, nature reserves and on some

some private lands where the landowners are committed to saving the Carolinian habitat. If your school is located in or near the Carolinian Forest Zone, try to arrange a field trip to view some of the typical Carolinian vegetation and perhaps even some of the designated species. Contact your local Natural Resources office or local conservation authority for help in planning an outing. Find out if any of the parents of your students own and maintain a Carolinian habitat that you could visit.

Plant A Tree

Planting trees is a very positive, hands-on project for students provided it is done properly and there is a plan in place for tree care once the trees are planted.

You don't need to wait until Arbor Day to plant a tree but spring or fall plantings are recommended. First you must find a place to plant your trees if your school property is not suitable. Contact your local conservation authority, town parks department or local Natural Resources office for ideas about where to plant, what to plant and how to ensure success. The following is a guide to planting your trees properly once you have them. Local media can be contacted to cover your conservation activity. This will not only instil excitement and pride in your class, but may also motivate other classes to do something too.

Activity

For the tree planting, you will need:
tree(s) 3 m tall or less (about 9')
shovels
burlap sack for each tree
twine
watering can
water
topsoil
peatmoss
wood chips (optional)
wooden stake
strips of cloth

— When you get your tree it is important to keep the root ball intact until the tree is planted. If no netting is already around the root ball, tie a damp burlap sack around the roots with some twine.

— Plant the tree as soon as possible. At the planting site, dig a hole in the ground a bit larger than the size of the root system. Water the empty hole generously.

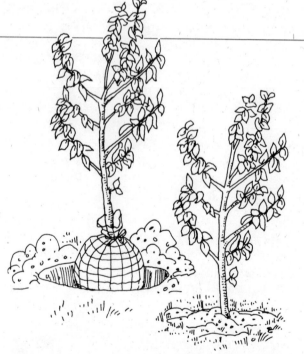

— Shovel about 15 cm (about 6'') of topsoil into the hole and place the roots in it. The burlap sack can stay on the tree as long as it is completely covered with soil. Any plastic or nylon mesh must be removed before planting.

48

— If your tree is over 120 cm tall (about 4') it should be supported with a wooden stake. Place the stake in the hole before completely filling it in with topsoil. Secure the stake to the tree trunk with strips of cloth tied loosely in a figure eight.

— Fill the hole with a mixture of topsoil and peatmoss (3:1). Tamp it down until it is firm and water well.

— After planting the tree, remove grass and other vegetation for 1 m (about 3') on all sides of the tree to reduce the competition for nutrients and water. Cover the exposed soil with wood chips or peat moss to help retain moisture around the tree.

— If it happens to be very dry, your tree may need extra watering.

After the tree-planting, have students brainstorm all the benefits their trees will provide.

Ask students to write a story about their tree-planting project.

Continue to visit the tree-planting location, either to maintain the trees (by mulching for example) or to add more trees, or to make use of the trees in your lessons. Pictures of the trees in different seasons can be taken.

LESSON 26

Waste Not, Want Not

For every 100 daily newspapers recycled, one tree is saved. Recycling is a terrific way to save trees, but cutting back on our uses of paper and paper products is even more important. Wasting paper is still a problem, even if it can be recycled later. This activity asks your students to think of all the ways that they can reduce their usage of paper and paper products.

If your school has a paper recycling program and you're already involved, terrific. If not, think about starting a recycling program in your school. You can contact your local Waste Management or Environmental Protection agency for information on what to do and a list of potential buyers for your recyclables.

Activities

1. Use Student Activity Sheet #27, "Waste Not, Want Not" to have students think of ways in which they can reduce the use of paper at school and at home. They can brainstorm the school part during class. Then they can take the activity home to complete the second part. Review everyone's suggestions.

2. Have students write a letter outlining how their family members could reduce their paper wastage, and possibly recycle more.

3. Have students write a letter to the editor of the local newspaper outlining their concerns and what they are presently doing to assist in the recycling program. Take pictures of the students involved in such a program.

A Tree Fair

Special events are an excellent way to teach children certain concepts. They learn not only from the final product, but also during the planning and set-up of the event, as well as its aftermath. Many skills, such as organizing, communicating, delegating and handling money are involved when planning a special event such as a fair. It takes time, commitment, and hard work but the results are usually tremendous. Your Tree Fair can be restricted to your class, a few grades at your school or you can make it a school-wide event and engage the help of other teachers and students in the preparation.

A Tree Fair can act as a summary of the concepts covered in this book. It can cover the basics of what trees are, how they grow and reproduce, what role trees play in nature, how trees affect people, why some trees are endangered and what everyone can do to help. Also, some of the crafts or projects done throughout the school year can be displayed at the fair.

Activity

If the whole school is involved, assign each class a subject on which to base their contributions to the fair. If only your class is hosting the fair, divide the students into working groups and assign (or have them choose) their topics. Contributions to the fair can take many forms. Examples include:

— displays using texts and illustrations, photographs, maps etc.

— games or puzzles for students to try

— food, using tree products

— models or other crafts and artwork

— creative writing such as stories, poems

— songs or skits

— a display of library books about trees

— newsclippings about trees

— display of tree products

— working experiments

— information about recycling

The class should plan together when the event will take place, where it will take place, and how it will be advertised. You may decide to charge a small admission fee, or sell some items, with money raised used to offset costs or to be donated to a conservation group. Decide how long the event should be and clear everything with the necessary authorities well in advance to avoid disappointment. If other classes are involved, the teachers should have a few planning meetings just to ensure that everyone is on track and knows what they are expected to do.

Contact local media — newspapers, radio, T.V. — for coverage of your event. When it's all over, write an account of what you did, how you did it, and how you'd improve a similar event next time. This will be invaluable for you and others in the future.

Student Activity Sheets

The Layers of a Tree

1. _____
2. _____
3. _____
4. _____
5. _____

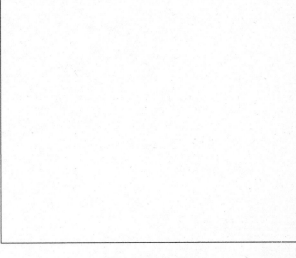

a slice of my tree model

1. _____
   _____
   _____
2. _____
   _____
   _____
3. _____
   _____
   _____
4. _____
   _____
   _____
5. _____
   _____
   _____

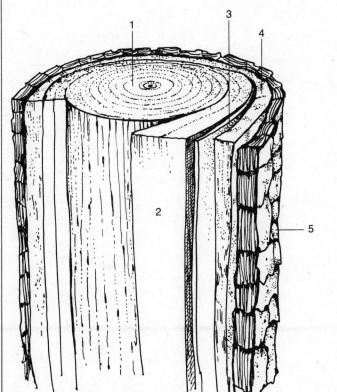

cross-section of a tree

Two Types of Trees

Using the words listed, fill in the different parts of the maple and pine trees.

Maple Tree
trunk
bark
roots
crown
broad leaf
flower
seeds

Pine Tree
trunk
bark
roots
crown
needle-like leaf
cone
seed

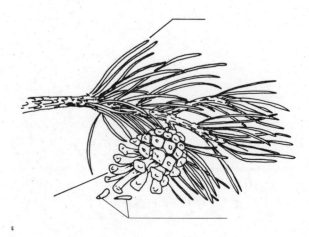

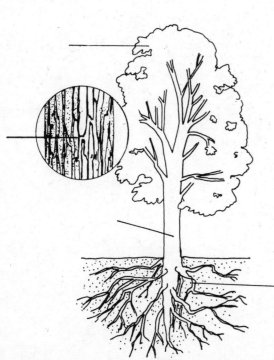

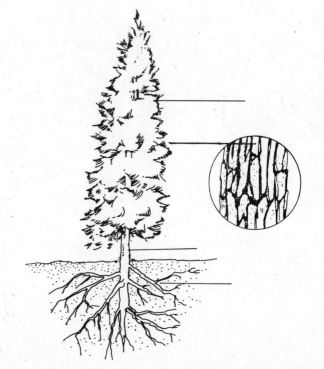

Looking at Leaf Shapes

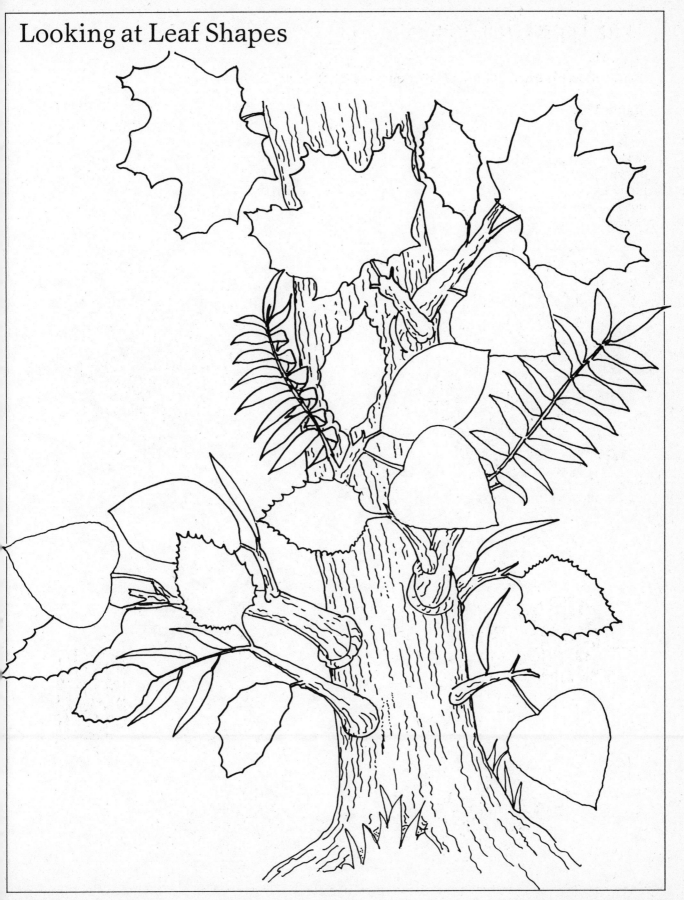

Looking at Leaf Shapes

Looking at Leaf Shapes

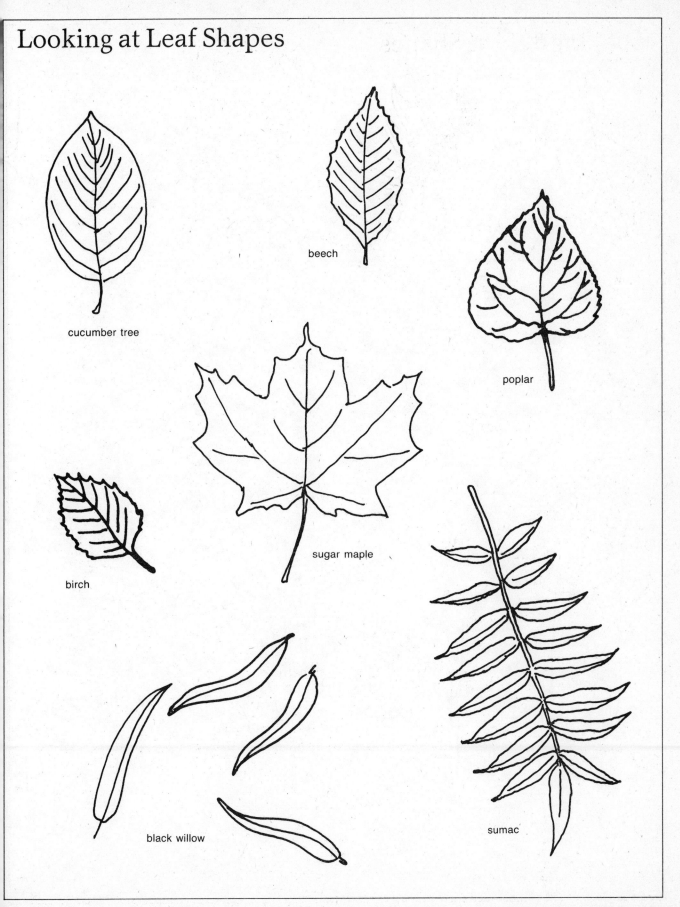

cucumber tree

beech

poplar

birch

sugar maple

black willow

sumac

Tree Teaser

Complete the tree names using the words in the forest.

1. ___ _a_ ___ ___ ___   5. ___ _i_ ___ ___ ___
2. ___ ___ _k_   6. ___ ___ ___ ___ _a_ ___
3. ___ _i_ ___ ___   7. ___ _p_ ___ ___ ___ ___
4. ___ ___ _r_ ___ ___   8. ___ ___ ___ ___ ___ ___ _a_ ___ ___

Tree Teaser

Use the shape codes to complete the names of trees.

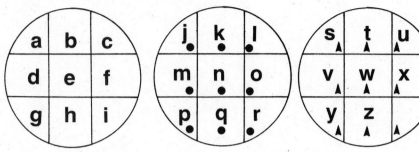

e l m

1.

2.

3.

4.

5.

6.

7.

8.

9.

10.

Tree Teaser

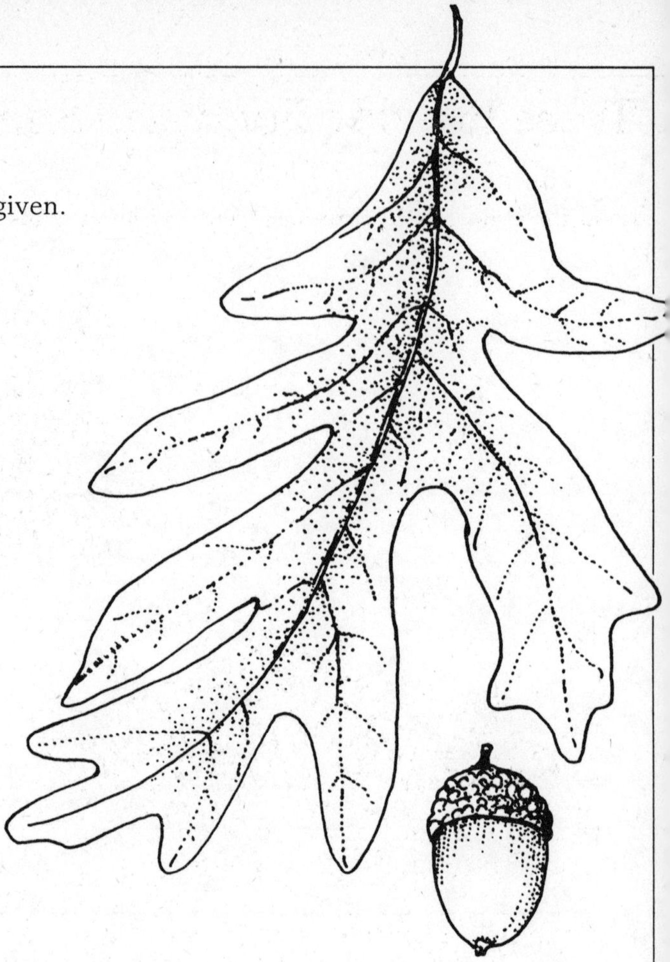

Find the name of a tree to rhyme with each word given.

Word **Rhyming Tree Name**

cash _____

search _____

helm _____

pillow _____

staple _____

purr _____

reach _____

mine _____

new _____

hairy _____

welder _____

choke _____

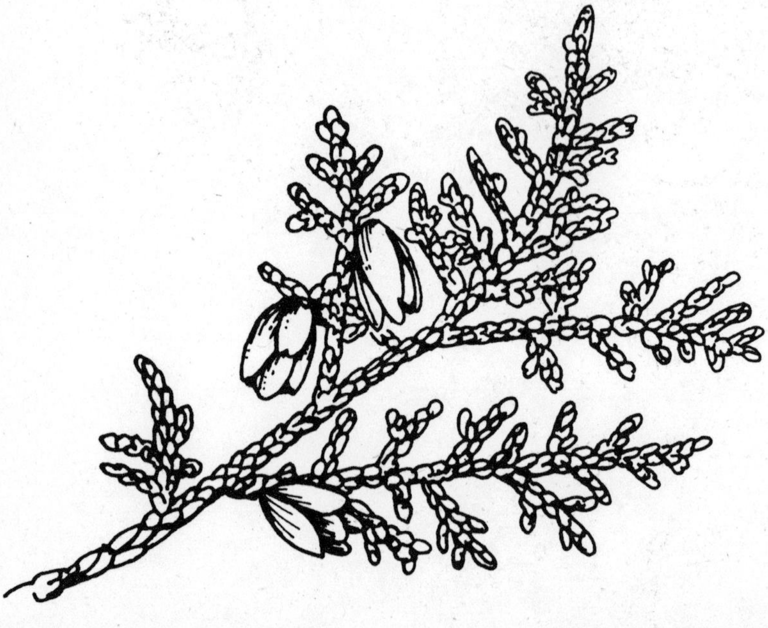

Trees Provide Food and Shelter

Look for clues left by animals. Identify the animals that have left clues.

Trees at Work

Look at the picture below and fill in the important "work" that trees are doing.

_____

_____

_____

_____

_____

_____

_____

Making Seeds

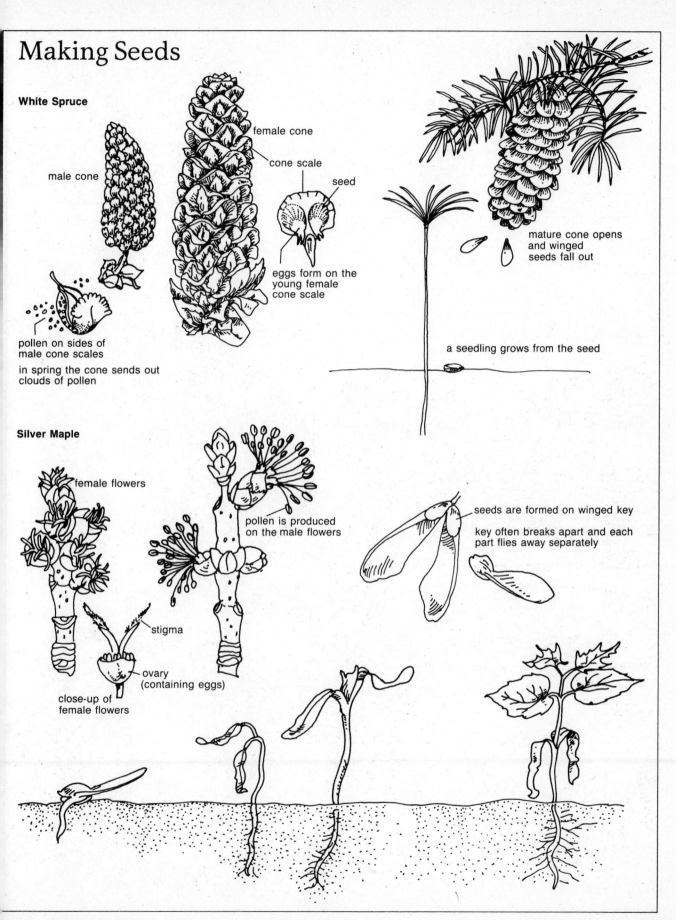

White Spruce

male cone

pollen on sides of
male cone scales

in spring the cone sends out
clouds of pollen

female cone

cone scale

seed

eggs form on the
young female
cone scale

mature cone opens
and winged
seeds fall out

a seedling grows from the seed

Silver Maple

female flowers

stigma

ovary
(containing eggs)

close-up of
female flowers

pollen is produced
on the male flowers

seeds are formed on winged key

key often breaks apart and each
part flies away separately

Seeds on the Move

Draw a connecting line between each seed and the way it travels to a new home.

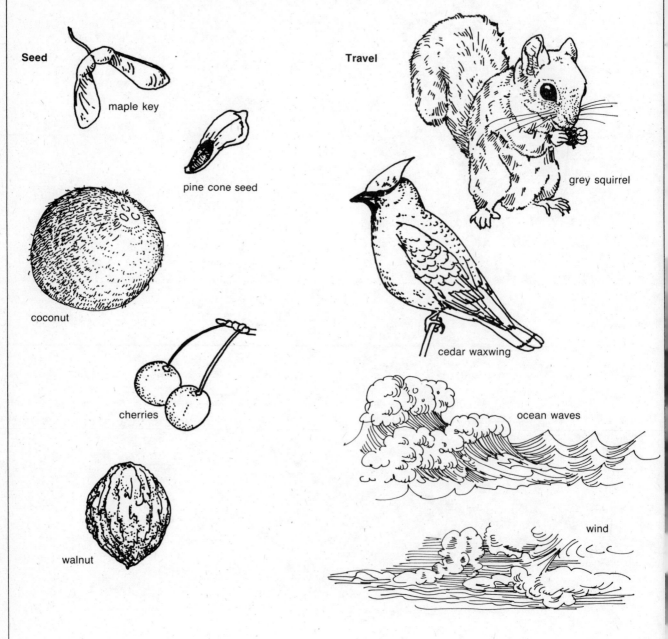

Seed

maple key

pine cone seed

coconut

cherries

walnut

Travel

grey squirrel

cedar waxwing

ocean waves

wind

Mini-Guide to Buds

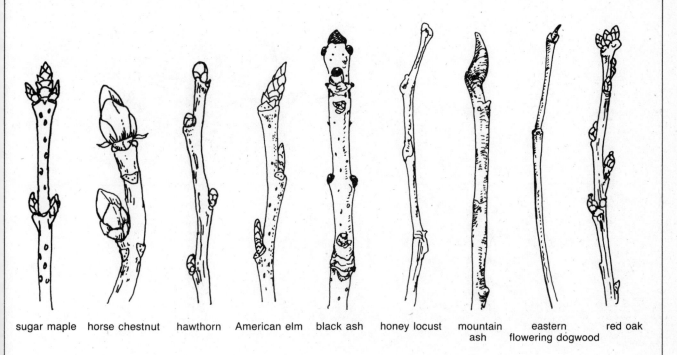

sugar maple   horse chestnut   hawthorn   American elm   black ash   honey locust   mountain ash   eastern flowering dogwood   red oak

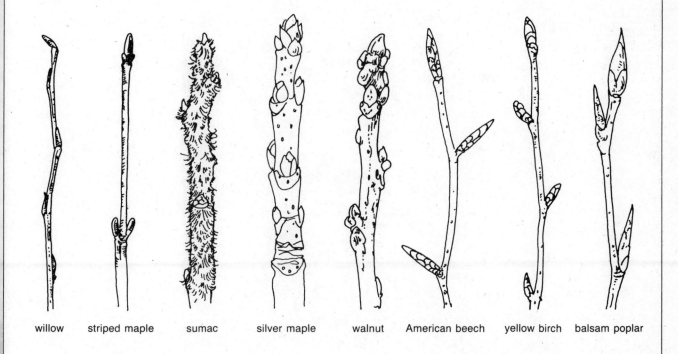

willow   striped maple   sumac   silver maple   walnut   American beech   yellow birch   balsam poplar

1

2

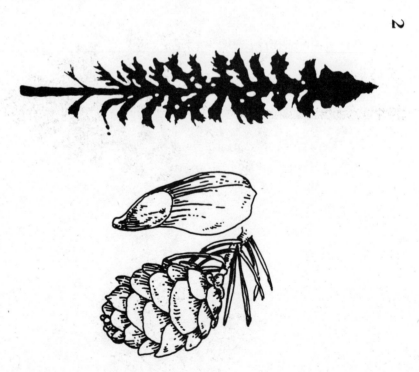

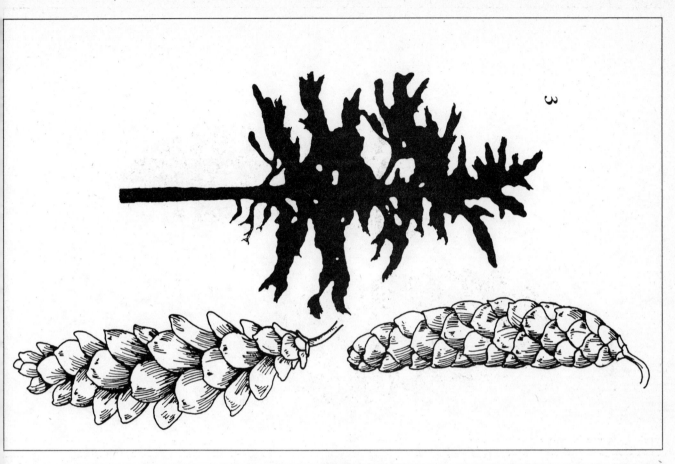

3

4

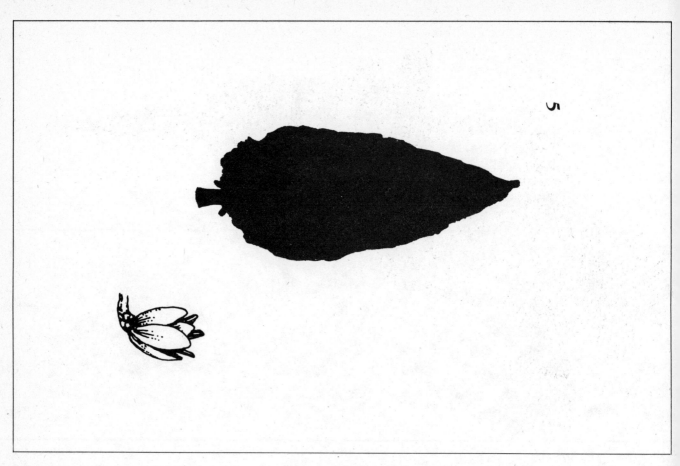

5

6

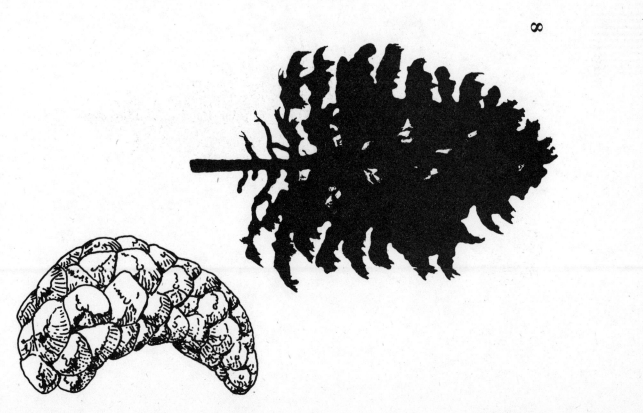

8

A Tree is our Home

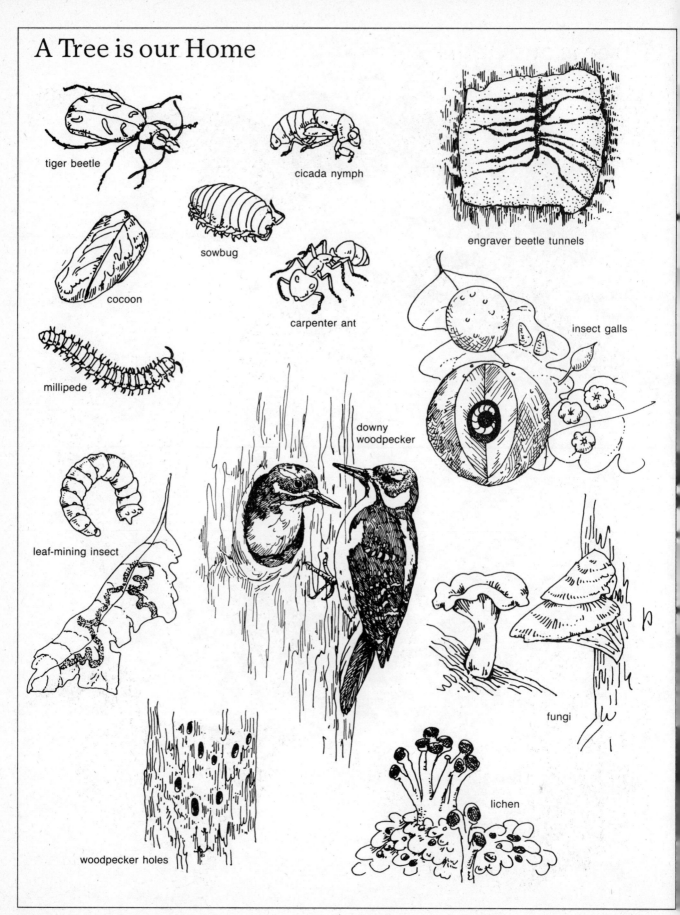

tiger beetle

cicada nymph

engraver beetle tunnels

sowbug

cocoon

carpenter ant

insect galls

millipede

downy woodpecker

leaf-mining insect

fungi

woodpecker holes

lichen

A Tree is our Home

weasel

kestrel

black-capped
chickadee

yellow-shafted
flicker

flying squirrel

grey squirrel
nest

opossum

wood duck

Cavity Nesters

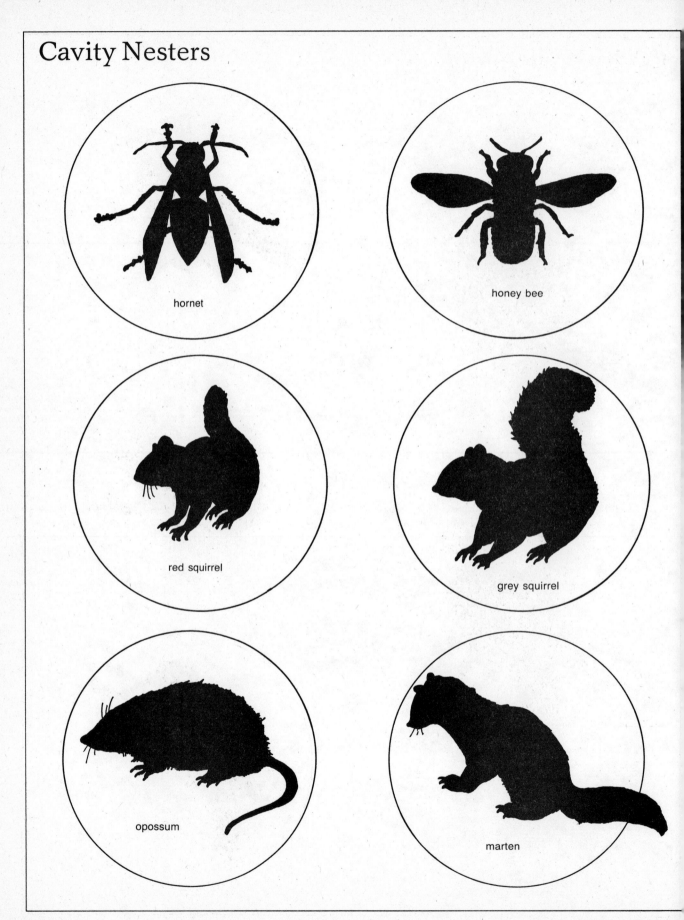

hornet

honey bee

red squirrel

grey squirrel

opossum

marten

Cavity Nesters

boreal owl

house sparrow

pileated woodpecker

tree frog

sapsucker

Cavity Nesters

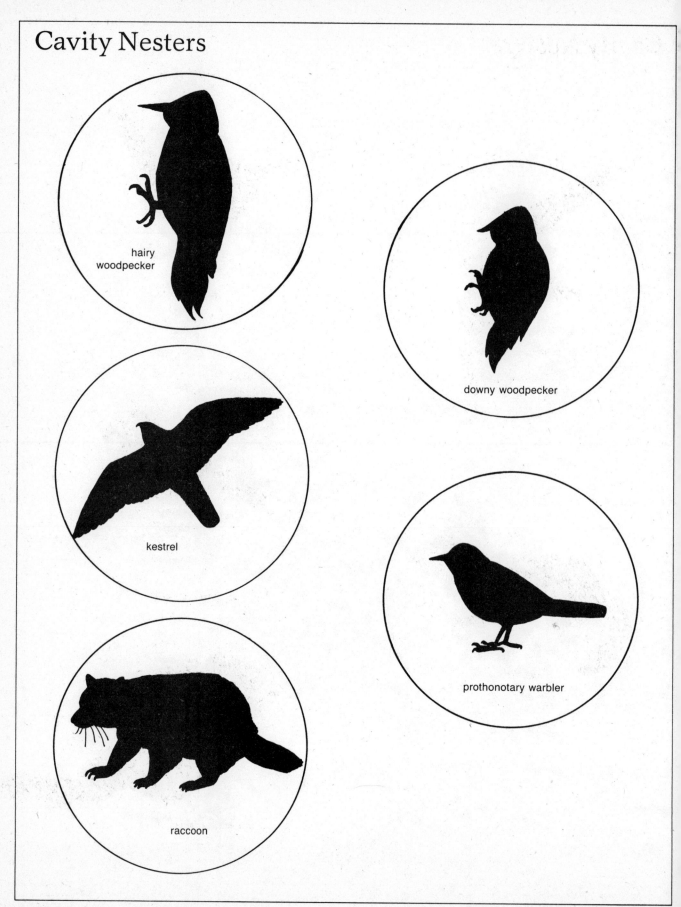

hairy
woodpecker

downy woodpecker

kestrel

prothonotary warbler

raccoon

Cavity Nesters

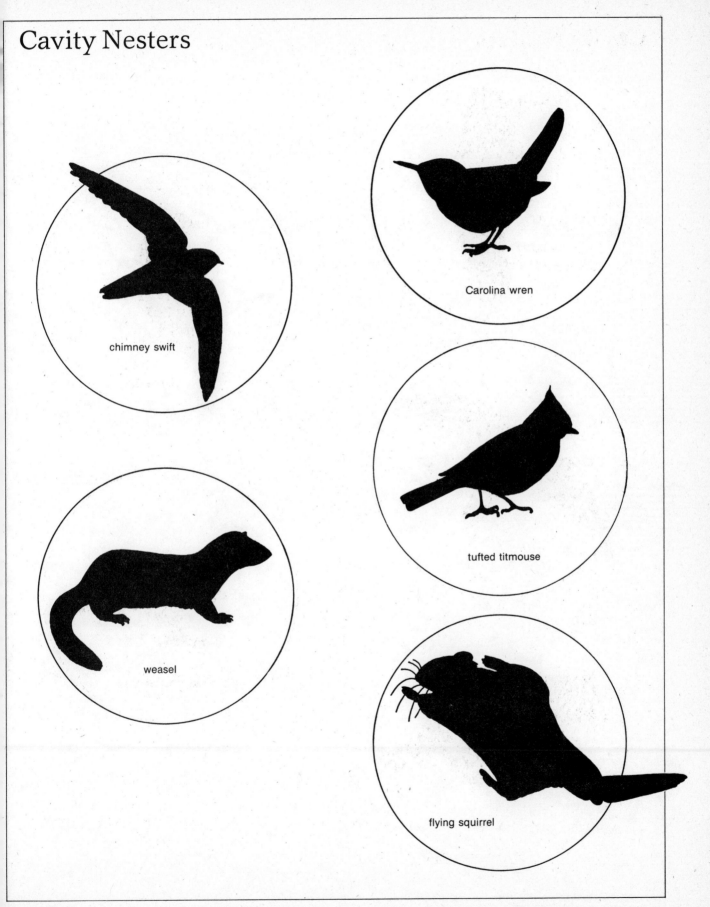

chimney swift

Carolina wren

tufted titmouse

weasel

flying squirrel

Cavity Nesters

barn swallow

nuthatch

wood duck

bufflehead

bluebird

Age a Tree

You can learn a lot about a tree by "reading" a cross-section of the trunk. What can you find out about the tree shown below? Look at the rings and then answer the questions below.

Questions

1. How old is the tree?

_____

2. How old was it during its best year of growth? How old was it when it grew the least in a year?

_____

3. What might have caused the tree to grow so little in that year?

_____

4. What might have caused the black scar you see?

_____

Trees And Me

A. Classroom Inventory

Things made from trees

Possible substitute materials

_____   _____
_____   _____
_____   _____
_____   _____
_____   _____
_____   _____
_____   _____
_____   _____

B. Now do the same activity at home in your bedroom.

Things made from trees

Possible substitute materials

_____   _____
_____   _____
_____   _____
_____   _____
_____   _____
_____   _____
_____   _____
_____   _____

A Tale of Two Forests

As you visit a managed and unmanaged forest today, fill in your observations on the sheet below.

Question	A. Managed Forest	B. Unmanaged Forest
What is your first impression of how the forest looks?		
What purposes does the forest serve?		
What signs of wildlife did you see?		
List some signs of forest management activity.		
List some signs that there has been no forest management activity.		

List the advantages and disadvantages of each type of forest.

Advantages   **Disadvantages**

Sharing the Land Roles

Forest Manager
It will be your job to explain the benefits of forest management, harvesting, and reforestation.

Government Official
You must consider all of the interests and decide what the government's priority is. You could think of and argue for a compromise.

Naturalist
You enjoy the natural beauty and wildlife of the forest and want to conserve it.

Biologist
You are concerned about the environmental and biological impacts of clearcutting the forest.

Native Leader
This forest is part of your band's cultural heritage and you are not willing to give it up.

Researcher
This forest represents one of the last stands of its kind in the region. It is an excellent site for research to help understand better how forest ecosystems work.

Forest Company Owner
You believe that the trees are very valuable and will be wasted if they're not cut. Clearcutting is the cheapest and most efficient way to do the job. You promise to replant the area so what's all the fuss about?

Recreationist
It doesn't really matter what happens to the forest as long as you'll still be able to skidoo or ride trail bikes there.

Town resident #1
It sounds like a good idea to cut the forest since there will be new jobs available in town and you'd like one of them. The forest is pretty but it doesn't pay your grocery bill.

Town resident #2
The forest is one of the only attractions of this town. If it goes, there will be no natural areas close by for walks, or just to enjoy looking at from the house.

Teacher
You've been using the forest as an outdoor classroom to teach your students about nature and conservation.

Photographer
The forest is one of your favorite places to take nature photos. You've even photographed some rare and threatened species here. If the forest goes, they'll go too.

Town resident #3
Although you like the forest as it is you think it has always been a fire hazard. Perhaps if it is cut down, replanted and managed properly, the risk of fire won't be a problem any more.

Developer
You've got another idea. You propose that the forestry company clear the land and make their money and then you will buy the land from the government and build a much needed shopping mall and subdivision.

Waste Not, Want Not

Did you know that for every 100 daily newspapers you recycle, you can save one tree? That's a lot of trees saved over a year. You can also help to save trees, not only by recycling, but also by reducing the amount of paper and paper products you use in the first place. Using the chart below, make a list of ways that you can cut back your paper use at school and at home.

At School

Kind of paper or paper product   alternative product   other ways to use less

e.g., note paper   write on both sides

_____

_____

_____

_____

_____

At Home

e.g. paper towels   washable cloth towels

_____

_____

_____

_____

_____

Fact Sheets

White Birch

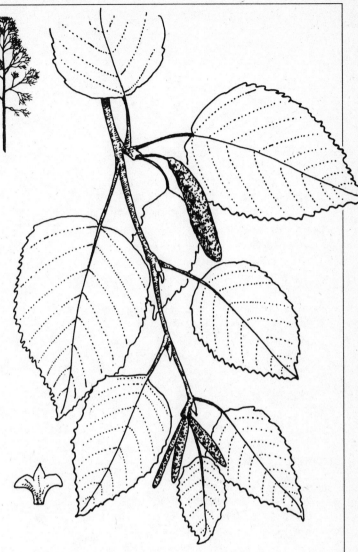

Look at Me:
— when growing in a forest the trunk is slender with a narrow, oval crown
— many small branches near the top
— adult trees have thin, creamy-white, papery bark that peels easily into sheets
— inner bark is reddish-orange
— simple, triangular, toothed leaves about 10 cm (about 4") long. Green leaves have a paler downy surface on their underside. The leaves turn yellow in autumn.
— greenish-brown buds are usually blunt and often gummy
— has separate male and female flowers, called catkins, on the same tree
— seeds are winged and wind dispersed

Size:
— a medium-sized tree
— grows up to 24 m (80') tall and 60 cm (2') in diameter

Find Me:
— grows in a variety of soil types but prefers well-drained sandy or silty loams
— cannot grow in the shade of other trees so it is often found growing in areas that have been burned over or clear-cut

I'm Special:
— although the tree is easily killed by fire due to its thin bark, it can quickly send up new shoots from around the base of its trunk and repopulate burnt over areas
— important wood for furniture, plywoods, veneers and pulpwood
— the bark was traditionally used by the native people for canoes, dishes, pots and pans, baskets, containers and many other essentials
— white birch is important to wildlife. The twigs serve as browse for moose and deer in winter, while beaver cut and feed on the innerbark. Grouse eat the buds and small birds and rodents feed on the tiny seeds.
— birch sap, when collected and boiled down, is sweet and delicious.

P.S.:
— tearing off the bark of white birch often kills the tree
— white birch is also called paper birch and canoe birch
— other birches include yellow birch, grey birch and, in Ontario, a single colony or grove of cherry birch

Words to Learn: catkin, clear-cut, crown, loam, pulpwood, veneer

American Beech

Look at Me:
— in the forest the trunk is often forked with a large crown
— simple elliptic leaves are 5-12 cm (2-4″) long and are dark bluish-green. The leaf veins are straight (not branching) and each one ends in a tooth. Leaves turn brown in fall and often stay on the tree during winter.
— thin, smooth, bluish-grey bark
— long, slender, pointy buds with four rows of scales
— nuts are formed in a reddish-brown, bristly husk that opens into four parts. There are two, three-sided nuts in each husk.
— male and female flowers are in separate clusters on the same tree.

Size:
— a large-sized tree
— grows up to 28 m (90′) high and up to 1.2 m (4′) in diameter

Find Me:
— a common tree in the Carolinian and Great Lakes-St. Lawrence Forest Zones
— often found growing with sugar maple, yellow birch and eastern hemlock
— prefers well-drained slopes and valleys

I'm Special:
— seedlings grow well in the shade of parent trees, often leading to a ''climax'' forest of maple-beech-hemlock that continues to replace itself until destroyed by fire or other disturbances
— nuts are edible for people and are also a favorite of black bears as well as squirrels, chipmunks, and ruffed grouse
— wood is used for flooring, furniture and hardware, such as handles. Specially treated beech wood is used for railway ties.
— pioneers used to stuff their mattresses with dried beech leaves intead of straw

P.S.:
— because of its smooth bark, people have often carved their initials in beech trees. Although the wounds may not kill the tree, they do provide holes in the bark where insects, fungi and diseases can enter the wood and harm the tree.
— despite its name, the blue beech is not related to the American beech

Words to Learn: crown, elliptic, fungi

Sugar Maple

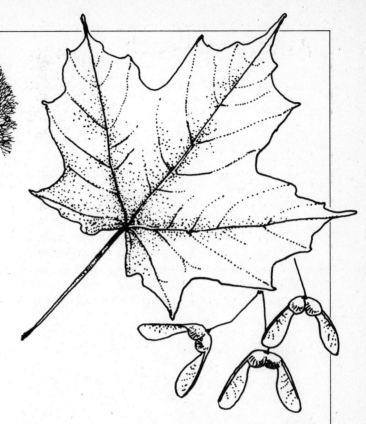

Look at Me:
- in the forest the trunk is straight with a rounded crown of short, sturdy branches
- simple, deep green leaves generally have five lobes with a few wavy teeth. The leaves are 7-12 cm (3-5″) across and turn yellow, bright orange or red in the fall.
- dark grey bark has long, irregular strips and appears rough
- reddish-brown buds are sharply pointed with slightly hairy scales
- pairs of seeds (sometimes called keys) are attached to long "wings" to help their dispersal by the wind
- small flowers appear like tassels on long stalks in spring

Size:
- one of the largest maples
- grows up to 27 m (80′) high and up to 80 cm (30″) in diameter but some have reached 40 m (130′) in height and 1.5 m (5′) in diameter

Find Me:
- prefers deep, rich, well-drained soils
- common in the Carolinian and Great Lakes-St. Lawrence Forest Zones
- very shade tolerant so it can reproduce successfully even in thick forests

I'm Special:
- its sap is the main source of maple syrup, an important industry; it takes about 40 L of sap to boil down to one litre of syrup.
- its wood is very valuable for furniture, flooring, veneer, plywood and other products
- birds and mammals eat the seeds, while whitetail deer feed on young twigs, buds and leaves. Grey squirrels and porcupines also eat branchlet tips.

P.S.:
- sometimes called rock maple because its wood is very hard
- the sugar maple leaf is found on the Canadian flag and Canadian penny and is an internationally recognized symbol of Canada
- other maples include: black maple, silver maple, red maple, mountain maple, striped maple and Manitoba maple.

Words to Learn: crown, lobes, veneer

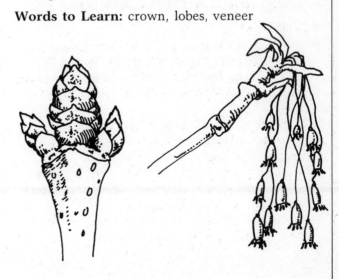

White Oak

Look at Me:
— when growing in a forest the trunk is long
  with no branches for about two-thirds of its
  height
— large, simple leaves are about 15 cm (6″) long
  and 7 cm (3″) wide. Leaves have 7-9 deep,
  narrow lobes with one or two blunt teeth.
  Leaves turn dark red in autumn and decom-
  pose very slowly once they have fallen.
— bark is light grey and scaly.
— fruit is an acorn, 1-2 cm (½-¾″) long, with a
  scale-covered cap over one end
— small, rounded buds are clustered about the
  ends of the twigs
— tiny flowers; male and female flowers grow
  separately on the same tree

Size:
— a large tree
— grows slowly, but can reach up to 30 m (100′)
  tall and 1.5 m (5′) in diameter

Find Me:
— grows well in deep, moist, well-drained soils
— found commonly in the Carolinian Forest
  Zone and in the southern parts of the Great
  Lakes-St. Lawrence Zone
— often grows with other oaks, basswood, black
  cherry, sugar maple, white ash or hickories

I'm Special:
— the acorn is an important source of food for
  wildlife including whitetail deer, raccoons,
  squirrels and quail
— oak trees provide excellent habitat for many
  species, including hundreds of kinds of insects
  and other invertebrates
— wood is very valuable for furniture, flooring,
  interior trim, boats and barrels
— oak trees are among the last trees to grow
  leaves in the spring and the last to drop their
  leaves in the fall

P.S.:
— acorns can be cooked and eaten
— oak trees are struck by lightning more often
  than any other kind of tree
— other oak trees include: bur oak, swamp
  white oak, Chinquapin oak, Shumard oak, red
  oak, black oak and northern pin oak
— oak apple galls are large, spongy, round swell-
  ings found on the leaves of some oaks. They
  are caused by gall flies invading the leaves.

Words to Learn: gall, invertebrate, lobes

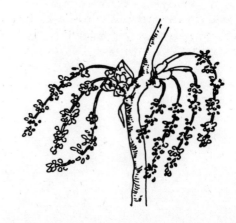

Black Ash

Look at Me:
— a slender, long trunk with a narrow crown of branches starting low on the trunk
— large, compound leaves are 25-40 cm (10-16") long and are divided into 7-11 oval leaflets. Leaflets have no stalks, are sharply toothed and are dark green.
— twigs are round and hairy
— pale grey, scaly bark is soft and corky. The ridges can be rubbed off easily by hand.
— small, flat seed is completely enclosed by the long, sometimes twisted seed wing. The wing helps the wind disperse the seed.
— dark brown to black buds are small
— flowers can be male, female or both in one (perfect) all on the same tree

Size:
— a small tree
— usually reaches 12-18 m (40-60') high and 30-60 cm (up to 2') in diameter

Find Me:
— grows in swampy woodlands
— found in Carolinian and Great Lakes-St. Lawrence forests, as well as in southern parts of the Boreal forest
— may grow together with white elm, eastern white cedar, red maple, speckled alder or silver maple.

I'm Special:
— wood is used for some furniture and interior trim
— wet wood can also be split vertically into thin slats and used for weaving baskets
— seeds are important food for wood ducks, grouse, many songbirds and small mammals. Whitetail deer and moose browse heavily on the twigs and young leaves.

P.S.:
— black ash is also called swamp ash
— other species of ash include white ash, red ash and blue ash (a threatened species)

Words to Learn: compound leaves, crown, leaflet, stalk, threatened species

Fact Sheet

Black Willow

Look at Me:
— depending on where it grows it can appear as a tree or shrub
— bark is dark brown to black with deep grooves
— pointed, narrow green leaves are about 7 cm (3") long and 1 cm (½") wide with a slight curve at the very tip
— young twigs are reddish-brown to pale orange
— flowers appear as catkins in the spring, with male and female flowers on different trees

Size:
— often considered to be the largest native willow in North America
— may range in height from 3-20 m (10-70')

Find Me:
— this willow is found along stream banks, lake shores and in swamps

I'm Special:
— the flowers are among the first to appear in the spring and are thought to be a very important food source for honey bees who depend on the pollen and nectar for food after a long winter
— black willow branches root easily and grow quickly; they are planted on eroding river banks so the roots can trap the soil and keep it from washing away
— wood is used for making polo balls

P.S.:
— there are about 75 different species of willow although most of them only reach shrub size
— the common pussy willow is a small tree. The small, fuzzy, whitish "pussies" are actually the female flowers just after they have burst from their buds

Words to Learn: catkin, eroding, polo

Black Spruce

Look at Me:
— when growing in a forest, the trunk grows straight without branching until near the top. The narrow crown consists of drooping branches with up-turned ends. The top of the tree often has a club-shaped, dense growth of branches that is easy to pick out at a glance.
— needle-like leaves are straight with a blunt end. They are evergreen and stay on the tree for five or more years.
— bark is dark greyish-brown, thin and scaly
— young twigs are covered with brownish hairs
— small, egg-shaped cones are found at the tips of branches. The cones do not drop from the tree in the fall but can stay on the tree for years, gradually opening and closing to release a few blackish, winged seeds at a time.
— small, greyish, pointed buds covered with fine hairs

Size:
— a small tree
— averages 9-15 m (30-50′) in height and 5-25 cm (2-10″) in diameter depending on where it is growing. Trees growing near the tree line in the north may only reach shrub size.

Find Me:
— grows in sphagnum bogs in the south to well-drained slopes in the north
— a typical species of the Boreal Forest, but it also grows in the Great Lakes-St. Lawrence Zone

I'm Special:
— black spruce can reproduce by seed and also by layering. This means that lower branches that become covered in mosses and decaying plant material can sprout roots and grow into new trees.

— loses its needles only a few at a time, like most conifers. The needles stay on the tree until the new needles have grown in, so you don't notice the loss.
— wood is very important in the pulp and paper industry
— in the far north, black spruce grows very slowly and a 20-40 year old tree may be only 1 m tall (about 3′)!

P.S.:
— black spruce may also be called bog spruce or swamp spruce
— other spruces include: white spruce and red spruce

Words to Learn: crown, layering, pulp, sphagnum, bog, tree line

Eastern White Pine

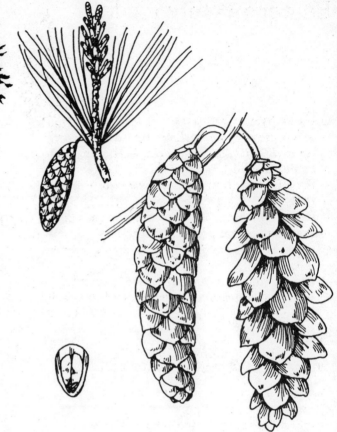

Look at Me:
— in the open the tree has wide-spreading branches growing straight out of the trunk
— in windy areas the branches tend to grow lop-sided on the tree, with the majority growing in the same direction as the wind blows
— needle-like leaves are 7-13 cm (2½-5″) long and grow in bunches of five
— evergreen
— cones are 7-20 cm (2½-8″) long
— old trees have dark greyish-brown bark with deep ridges while young trees have smooth greyish-green bark

Size:
— a large tree
— tallest conifer in eastern areas, often growing to 30 m (100′) and reaching 1 m (3′) in diameter

Find Me:
— it is a typical tree of the Great Lakes-St. Lawrence Forest Zone and is also found in the southern part of the Boreal Forest Zone and west of Lake Superior and in the Carolinian Zone
— grows best on moist sandy or loamy soils, although it can be found growing on rocky ridges and in bogs

I'm Special:
— it has five needles in a clump and is easily identified by remembering that each needle stands for one letter in its name: W-H-I-T-E
— the branches grow in one whorl each year, so by counting the spaces between the whorls you can estimate the age of the tree
— black-capped chickadees, red crossbills and other birds feed on the seeds found in the cones
— this is a valuable tree species for softwood lumber. It is used for trim, panelling, siding and cabinet work.

— early settlers made their log cabins as well as many of their furnishings from white pine
— in the early 1800's, logging of white pine was an important industry. The timbers were used for the British shipbuilding industry.

P.S.:
— the white pine is Ontario's official tree
— windblown white pines were often the subjects of paintings by Canada's famous Group of Seven
— other pines include: red pine, jack pine and pitch pine

Words to Learn: bog, conifer, evergreen, loam

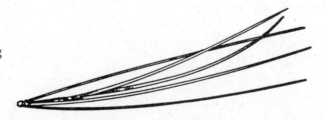

Eastern White Cedar

Look at Me:
— when growing in an open area it has a narrow, cone-shaped crown, branching almost to the ground
— the trunk is often divided into two or more parts
— dense foliage
— scale-like leaves are yellowish-green
— small, oval cones are 5 mm-1.5 cm (¼-½″) long
— bark is thin and reddish-brown. On older trees it forms long, thin strips that are easily peeled off.

Size:
— a small to medium-sized tree
— averages 14 m (45′) tall and 30 cm (1′) in diameter

Find Me:
— grows throughout the Great Lakes-St. Lawrence Forest Zone and is also found in the Boreal and northern Carolinian Zones
— prefers swampy areas over a limestone bedrock
— also grows in shallow dry soils as well as in shallow bogs

I'm Special:
— wood is very resistant to rot and is commonly used for posts, poles, fences, shingles and canoes
— wood has a strong aroma that is known to discourage insects so cedar is often used to line blanket boxes, closets and clothes chests to keep out moths and other damaging insects

— instead of shedding individual leaves like most trees, it sheds entire lateral branchlets, leaves and all, from old parts of the branches
— the eastern white cedar is a popular ornamental tree and is commonly used in hedges because of its thick foliage

P.S.:
— the native people used its bark to make rope
— this tree is not a true ''cedar'' but is really a species of Arbor-vitae (tree of life)
— despite its name, eastern red cedar is not related to eastern white cedar. It belongs to the juniper family.

Words to Learn: bedrock, bog, foliage

Tamarack

Look at Me:
— when growing in a forest the tree has a straight trunk with a narrow, cone-shaped crown
— twigs are orangish-brown. There are two types of twigs: elongated ones on the ends of branches and dwarf ones farther back on the branches.
— needle-like, light green leaves are about 2.5 cm (1″) long and turn yellow in autumn. Leaves grow singly on the elongated twigs but in clusters of 10-20 on the dwarf twigs (*see* illustration).
— small, light brown cones are about 1.5 cm (½″) long and stay on the tree all winter
— older trees have reddish-brown, scaly bark
— inner bark is bright reddish-purple

Size:
— a small to medium-sized tree
— grows from 9-20 m (30-65′) tall and 30-60 cm (1-3′) in diameter

Find Me:
— has a wide range extending from the Carolinian Zone to the tundra
— grows in cold, wet, poorly drained areas such as swamps and bogs
— cannot grow in shade

I'm Special:
— one of the few conifers to drop all of its needles in the fall
— wood is used for railway ties, poles, posts, boxes, crates, boat-building and pulpwood
— bark contains tannin which is used for tanning leather

P.S.:
— tamarack is also known as hackmatack or eastern larch

Words to Learn: bog, conifer